THE STORY OF

THE DECLARATION OF INDEPENDENCE

THE STORY  OF

Pictures by HIRST MILHOLLEN and MILTON KAPLAN

New York

Bicentennial Edition

THE *Declaration of Independence*

Text by DUMAS MALONE

☆ OXFORD UNIVERSITY PRESS ☆ *1975*

Dedicated to our colleague
HIRST DILLON MILHOLLEN
(1906–1970)
etcher, historian, photographer,
who was a pioneer both in
pictorial research and
pictorial documentation

CONTENTS

PART *One*

THE DECLARATION THEN

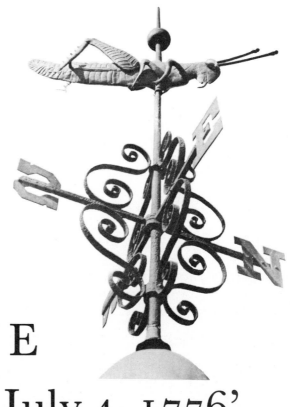

PROLOGUE
'In Congress, July 4, 1776'

THE birthday of the United States of America was bright and pleasant. At six a.m. on the fourth of July, 1776, Thomas Jefferson, one of the delegates from Virginia to the Continental Congress in Philadelphia and a man who was always enormously interested in wind and weather, noted that the temperature was 68 degrees Fahrenheit. The wind was southeast and the mercury rose to 76 in the heat of the day, which was not at all bad for the season. Forty or fifty representatives from what had been called provinces or colonies, from New Hampshire to Georgia, had been meeting for some time in Pennsylvania's brick State House —later to be known as Independence Hall— and on this day their debates did not end till evening.

The story is that an old bellman had been in the steeple since the delegates gathered in the morning; he was waiting for a signal from a boy stationed at the door below. On the bell in this steeple was an inscription from Leviticus: 'Proclaim liberty throughout all the land unto all the inhabitants thereof.' A declaration of liberty was expected from the patriots who were gathered here, and the old man hastened to proclaim it when the boy below clapped his hands and shouted, 'Ring! Ring!' This was the signal of the birth of the Republic dedicated to the freedom of the human spirit and destined to power beyond men's dreams.

A resolution of political independence had been adopted two days earlier, and John Adams, a delegate from Massachusetts, supposed that the second of July would be celebrated by later generations of grateful Americans. He wrote his wife, Abigail: 'It ought to be celebrated, as the day of deliverance, by solemn acts of devotion to God Almighty. It ought to be solemnized with pomp and parade, with shows, games, sports, guns, bells, bonfires, and illuminations, from one end of this continent to the other, from this time forward, evermore.' But the birth certificate of the infant Republic bore the date July fourth, when a full charter of freedom was finally and formally approved. The Declaration of Independence was more than a fateful political resolution; it embodied a timeless philosophy and an undying faith.

Not long afterward the fanciful tale was told overseas that the Congress, after declaring the colonies independent states, placed a Crown on the Bible and offered this to God. Then, after the religious ceremony, the Crown was divided into thirteen parts and distributed. It would have been more correct to say that the delegates, discarding a Crown they would have no part in,

placed the Declaration on the Bible, thus investing this first great charter of a nation with the sanctity it has ever since retained.

Although it rightly became a sacred charter, it was nonetheless a human document—prepared and adopted under particular circumstances not by angels or demigods, but by living men. Thereby hangs a tale and an engrossing one. How did these things come about and what did these words mean? What manner of men pledged to this cause their lives, their fortunes, and their sacred honor? What has happened to the work of their minds and hands in the intervening years? What has become of the immortal Declaration? Does it still warm the hearts and quicken the blood of men? Such questions we shall try to answer here in words and pictures.

A, N.W. VIEW OF THE STATE HOUSE IN PHILADELPHIA taken 1778

Two years after the Congress declared for independence, Charles Willson Peale made this northwest view of the Pennsylvania State House and its wooden sheds. Tradition has it that in earlier years visiting Indian delegations were housed in one of the sheds.

4

Causes which IMPELLED

THE Declaration of Independence proclaimed the advent of a potentially great Republic. It also marked the end of a long chain of political events and placed the seal of approval on a revolt which had been for some months in process. The appeal to argument had already given way to the appeal to arms, and blood had been shed at Lexington and Concord and Bunker Hill. But, as John Adams reminded his old friend Thomas Jefferson when both of them were aged, the real revolution occurred in 'the minds of the people' before the clash of arms. He set the date for its beginnings in 1760—the year that George III became King, and Jefferson went to the College of William and Mary, and the French surrendered Canada.

Now that we can look back at this revolution through the generations, it seems to have started long before that. It began in the spirit of liberty which was brought by the colonists to the remote shores of a fresh continent and was nourished by the relatively independent lives they lived here. The Americans would hardly have sought full freedom if they had not previously enjoyed a high degree of personal and political liberty and had not already become habituated to local self-government. In New England towns and in Southern counties, in the Massachusetts General Court and the Virginia House of Burgesses, colonial Americans had grown accustomed to the control of their own lives and the management of their own affairs. Occasionally they had suffered from despotic royal governors, but rarely was there a question of their rights and privileges and immunities as freeborn Englishmen.

In the far-flung British Empire the colonies were subordinate to the mother country and were expected to contribute to her welfare, but the imperial tie rested lightly on most Americans and they were far from subservient in spirit. A visitor among the polite planters of Virginia toward the end of the French and Indian War, while noting that they were characteristically a generous and loyal people, had this to say about their public character: 'They are haughty and jealous of their liberties, and can scarcely bear the thought of being controlled by any superior power.'

The simplest explanation of the revolt of the Americans is that they had attained such ma-

LOCAL TOWN MEETINGS *fostered independence of spirit. In 1774 Parliament attempted to curb those in Massachusetts because 'the inhabitants have, contrary to the design of their institution, been misled to treat upon matters of the most general concern, and to pass many dangerous and unwarranted resolves.'*

turity and self-reliance by the end of the successful British struggle against the French that they resented the degree of control which the mother country sought to impose upon them in the postwar period; and that they left the family roof after a family quarrel, assuming the equal station among the Powers of the earth to which they now believed themselves entitled. On the other hand the mother country, showing a not uncommon parental blindness to increased maturity, had sought for her own purposes to impose fresh restrictions at just the time that

WILLIAM PITT, *the elder, first Earl of Chatham, opposed the Government's harsh American policies and advocated milder measures.*

7

GEORGE III *ascended the throne, and*
Thomas Jefferson entered college, in 1760.

WILLIAMSBURG *was the seat of the Virginia House of Burgesses.*

S.W. View of the STATE-HOUSE, in *BOSTON.*

Seat of government in Boston was the Town-house. When Bostonians began calling it 'the State House,' Sir Francis Bernard, Royal Governor of Massachusetts, irritably said that the name exaggerated the importance of the representative bodies that met there.

the colonists saw little further need for her protection. Thus she had precipitated a crisis.

The fateful quarrel began when the home government, bearing the burdens and facing the problems of an enlarged empire, sought to gain increased revenue from the colonies—which were in fact major beneficiaries of the great victory over the French. First the British officials attempted to gain better enforcement of the existing trade laws. Then, directly and indirectly, they sought to tax the colonies. Meeting resistance at every turn, they finally attacked the colonial governments themselves. In the course of the dispute, colonial leaders such as Benjamin Franklin, John Adams, Thomas Jefferson, and James Wilson of Pennsylvania proposed what amounted to a dominion status, but the British statesmanship of the era was incapable of rising to the occasion as it did in the case of Canada in the next century. Because of official stupidity and the mulish stubborness of King George III himself, the issue finally became one between freedom and coercion, and it was in the name of political liberty and personal rights that the Americans took up their arms.

A Train of ABUSES

A FLAME IS LIGHTED IN THE BAY COLONY

B Y 1776 Americans looked back on the era of the old Navigation Laws as a time of joyous youthful freedom. This came to an end when the mother country sought to tighten imperial control and enforce trade regulations which had been long evaded. Naturally the efforts of the home government met with special resistance in commercial New England, which had profited considerably from official laxity.

In the province of Massachusetts Bay in the early 1760's, Writs of Assistance became a burning issue. These were search warrants issued by courts, and royal officials sought them in the effort to run down violators of the customs laws. Smuggling was by no means uncommon among the thrifty and ingenious Yankees. For example, they frequently brought in molasses from the French West Indies without paying the duty and then made this into rum, which could be pleasantly imbibed or conveniently used in further trading. But these writs were objected to as unwarranted infringements on individual privacy and freedom, and unquestionably they were liable to grave abuse.

James Otis, a brilliant lawyer, gained deserved fame by his powerful arguments against

JAMES OTIS *told Bostonians cele-brating the end of the French and Indian War that the true interests of Great Britain and her colonies were identical. But a short time later he was a leader of the American patriots.*

the Writs of Assistance before the superior court of the province. Describing him as a 'flame of fire,' John Adams said: 'American independence was then and there born; the seeds of patriots and heroes were then and there sown.' Otis lost his case in the first instance but was afterward sustained, and he remained for some years the leader of the patriot party in the colony. His public career came to an untimely end in 1769, when a Crown official struck him over the head with a cutlass and unhinged his reason. He lived until American independence had been gained, finally being struck by lightning; though not a Signer of the Declaration, he was indubitably a Father of the Republic.

This is the Place to affix the STAMP.

NO TAXATION WITHOUT REPRESENTATION

BETTER KNOWN than the Writs of Assistance, which Otis so strongly contested in Massachusetts, was the Stamp Act, which was opposed by practically everybody in all the colonies. This was the first direct tax that Parliament had ever imposed on the Americans and there were strong theoretical grounds for objection to it. This was no mere matter of the control of external commerce but of internal taxation. Hence the cry which resounded in England as well as America: 'No taxation without representation.' The purpose of the Act was the legitimate one of meeting part of the cost of the British military establishment in America, but the colonists were either indifferent to or opposed to that, and there were particular objections to this tax. It fell on newspapers, legal papers of all sorts, ships' papers, even on playing cards. The stamps were visible objects of wrath and the most articulate groups—the editors and lawyers—were directly affected.

The Stamp Act was passed in March 1765, but it was not to become effective until November and there was plenty of time to fulminate against it. In the proud Virginia House of Burgesses in May, Patrick Henry made a famous speech in which he said that Caesar had

With broadsword in hand, the Earl of Bute prepares to kill America, the goose that laid the golden eggs. Bute often received the attention of the British cartoonists who attributed the measures against the Colonies to his influence.

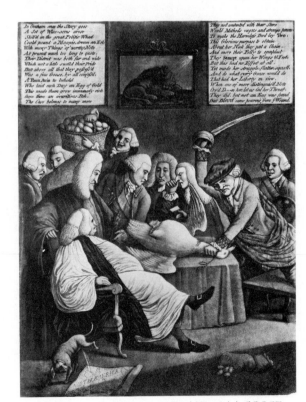

THE WISE MEN of GOTHAM and their GOOSE

THE STAMP ACT *provoked mob action. From Massachusetts to the Carolinas men rebelled against the Act.*

his Brutus and Charles I his Cromwell, but was interrupted by cries of 'Treason' when he uttered the name of King George III. There is some uncertainty about what he said next, but young Thomas Jefferson, a law student in Williamsburg, who was listening in the lobby of the Burgess chamber, gained an indelible impression of sublime eloquence. He never had any doubt that the impassioned orator then and there became the leader of protest in the oldest and largest of the provinces.

The 'forest-born Demosthenes' introduced certain resolutions on this occasion which got into the mails in advance, excited heated newspaper comment as far away as Boston, and sounded the alarm bell of revolution a decade before revolution actually took place. One of these resolutions boldly asserted the exclusive right of the Assembly to levy taxes and stated that the attempt to vest such power in any other person or persons whatsoever had a manifest tendency to destroy both British and American freedom. This was a direct slap at Parliament which the older leaders thought unnecessary at the time, since they had already made dignified remonstrance against the Act itself. But Henry captivated the 'young hot and giddy members,' as he did young Jefferson. Ultimately, the extreme resolution was expunged but the word had gone forth that Parliament had been openly defied.

In the autumn, when the Act was supposed to go into effect, there was relative quiet in Virginia, chiefly because the popular governor, Francis Fauquier, frankly recognized that it was unenforceable. Things were different in that other major seat of disaffection, the province of Massachusetts Bay, where Sir Francis Bernard, the governor, and Lieutenant-Governor Thomas Hutchinson were not so popular. Hutchinson, a learned and conservative man, who symbolized loyalty to the Crown during this stormy decade, was disposed to blame the discontent and disorder on Samuel Adams. Adams was no impassioned orator like Patrick Henry, but he was incessantly active behind the scenes, and he ranks with Otis and Henry

Aristocratic Sir Francis Bernard was governor of New Jersey before becoming governor of Massachusetts Bay in 1760. His devotion to royal policy was rewarded with a baronetcy, and hastened the war.

as a forerunner of independence if he does not overtop them both.

In the Bay Colony, the struggle against the British assumed to some extent the character of class conflict—between the popular party and the aristocratic party centering in the governor and his court. Rich young John Hancock, who came into his estate about this time, did not become a conspicuous patriot until a few years later. Samuel Adams, who was forty-three in the year of the Stamp Act and already looked like an old man though he did not act like one, was definitely identified with the popular party from the beginning. This Harvard graduate, who showed as great indifference to his private affairs as he did zeal in all public matters, was already a man of considerable political influence in Boston before the crisis in imperial relations occurred. Hutchinson had no doubt whatever that Sam Adams did everything possible to accentuate this crisis, and eventually the

13

14

The House of Burgesses in the restored capitol at Williamsburg as it appeared when Patrick Henry delivered his famous speech.

Aroused by the Stamp Act, Patrick Henry made a stirring speech in the House of Burgesses. Cries of treason interrupted him as he said, 'Caesar had his Brutus, Charles I his Cromwell, and George III . . .' Shown here is a romanticized painting of the mid-nineteenth century.

SAMUEL ADAMS, who met with fellow liberty lovers at the Green Dragon tavern, was a born agitator dedicated to the cause he believed right.

JOHN HANCOCK *did not hesitate to risk his fortune by supporting the colonial cause.*

Lieutenant-Governor described his foe as a man of malignant heart and a supreme incendiary. To the colonial patriots, on the other hand, this artful but simple man seemed an untiring friend of the popular interest and a selfless and dauntless champion of colonial rights. He had no superior as an agitator and manager, and the events of 1764–1765 gave him a supreme opportunity.

The Sugar Act of 1764 had preceded the Stamp Act and inaugurated the policy associated with the name of George Grenville, Chancellor of the Exchequer. While nominally a trade measure it was really designed to raise revenue rather than to regulate commerce. In the 'Caucus Club,' which met in a smoke-filled garret, Adams had devised means for calling public attention to the real nature of this law, while James Otis was assailing it on legal grounds. But it had aroused no such general objections as the Stamp Act. The latter led to the organization of 'Sons of Liberty' in Boston and other towns. The more extreme anti-British elements were in these organizations, and they were not averse to a little rioting.

This elaborate cartoon celebrated the repeal of the Stamp Act by depicting its burial at the water's edge.

Glorious News:

Conſtitutional LIBERTY Revives!

In the month of August, in Boston, the effigy of Andrew Oliver, brother-in-law of Hutchinson and appointee to the lucrative post of stamp officer, was hung from the greatest of a group of elms at the corner of the present Washington and Essex Streets. Under these elms the crowds were accustomed to gather and this elm became famous as the 'Liberty Tree.' Mr. Oliver's fence was also pulled down and that unhappy gentleman resigned his exceedingly unpopular position. A few days later, Hutchinson's house was gutted by rioters and his valuable books and papers were scattered in the streets. This wanton act caused many to believe that the advocates of colonial rights had been too zealous.

But the net result of the activities in Boston and elsewhere was the wholesale resignation of stamp collectors throughout the colonies and the complete inability of the British government to enforce the law. Parliament repealed it for obvious practical reasons, but that body passed at the same time (1766) the Declaratory Act, which asserted the right to legislate for the colonies in 'all cases whatsoever.' This claim should never have been asserted since it would not be conceded except under extreme compulsion.

THE SAME MEDICINE IN ANOTHER BOTTLE

THE NEXT STAGE in the unfolding controversy was marked by the passage of the Townshend Acts (1767), as they are called in the history books. Nominally these were laws in regulation of commerce but actually, as the showy and cynical British minister who instigated them admitted, their main purpose was the procuring of revenue. Deriding the distinction between internal and external taxes, Charles Townshend said that since the colonists objected to the one he would give them the other. Thereby he made a mistake, for he inevitably caused clear-headed Americans like Franklin and Jefferson to assert in due course that Parliament had no right to impose either. As a practical measure the new

duties on glass, paper, colors, and tea bore most heavily on the more commercial colonies; and indignation was great in Boston, where a board of customs commissioners was now seated and Samuel Adams in season and out of season was inciting the spirit of resistance.

Early in 1768 the House of Representatives of Massachusetts Bay, which was now controlled by the 'radicals,' sent to the other colonies a circular letter which Samuel Adams drew. In this they urged united action against the Townshend duties. The British government unwisely made an issue of this, instructing the various royal governors to dissolve any Assembly that approved the circular. Several assem-

18

CHARLES TOWNSHEND, *Chancellor of the Exchequer, did not live to see Britain reap the results of his cynical revenue measures.*

blies had already approved it; and the House of Burgesses of Virginia passed resolutions of their own, solemnly declaring that they, and not Parliament, had the right to levy taxes on the colony. These led to the dissolution of the Assembly by the genial governor, Lord Botetourt, who would have liked to avoid this crisis. The 'late representatives of the people' then proceeded to Raleigh Tavern and adopted an 'Association,' based in part on a draft by scholarly George Mason which his neighbor George Washington had brought to the meeting in his pocket. This was a non-importation, non-consumption agreement, similar to those adopted in many colonies, but it was specially significant because of the importance of Virginia and the character of the men involved

In New York merchants met at Burns's tavern on Broadway and decided to boycott British goods until the Stamp Act was repealed.

Virginians, meeting in Raleigh Tavern, agreed to boycott British goods.

49

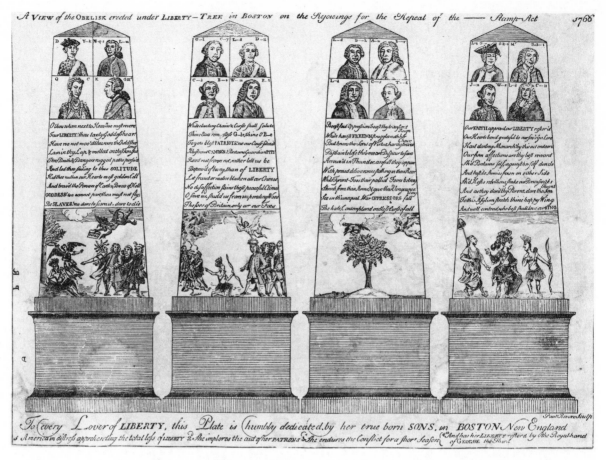

On May 19, 1766, *The Boston Gazette and Country Journal carried an announcement that, to celebrate the repeal of the Stamp Act, an obelisk will be exhibited on the Common, 'A description of which is engraved by Mr. Paul Revere: and is now selling by Edes and Gill.'*

THE NEW *MASSACHUSETTS*

LIBERTY SONG,

[*To the Tune of the British Grenadier.*]

TO all Gentlemen VOLUNTEERS,

who prefer LIBERTY to SLAVERY, and are hearty Friends to the GRAND *AMERICAN* CAUSE; who are free and willing to serve this STATE, in the Character of a

CADWALLADER COLDEN, *governor of New York, strongly opposed colonial independence.*

in it. These landed gentry were under the influence of no city mob, but they had asserted their 'rights' and stood shoulder to shoulder with the patriots of Boston and the merchants of the commercial centers such as New York, where the royal lieutenant-governor, Cadwallader Colden, was also troubled by riotous Sons of Liberty.

The repeal of the Townshend Acts was inevitable because they had proved unenforceable, and Lord North, who was now the head of the Ministry, brought it about; but just to show its authority Parliament left the tax on tea. This remained as a hated symbol and patriotic leaders continued to inveigh against it, especially in Massachusetts. But resentment declined in most places and the non-importation agreements were gradually given up. Several years of relative calm ensued, though there was a famous incident in Boston. This is known in history and legend as the 'Boston Massacre,' though it hardly deserved that name.

UNION, ACTIVITY and FREEDOM,
O R,
DIVISION, SUPINENESS and SLAVERY.

To all the good PEOPLE
O F
VIRGINIA.

BRITISH WARSHIPS *disembarked infantry and cannon in Boston at the beginning of October 1768 for police duty. The troops 'landed on the Long Wharf; there Formed and Marched with insolent Parade, Drums beating, Fifes playing, and Colours flying, up King Street, Each Soldier having received 16 rounds of Powder and Ball.'*

MASSACRE IN BOSTON

BEFORE THE REPEAL of the Townshend Acts, two regiments of British regulars had been brought to this seat of disaffection—in order 'to rescue the Government from the hands of a trained mob,' according to Governor Bernard. That is, the redcoats, or 'lobsterbacks,' were intended as a police force and a sort of army of occupation. That they would be received with sullen resentment by the populace and become the object of jeers and badgering was inevitable. Their officers tried to keep these ill-paid and relatively idle soldiers in hand but some of them were villainous, and there were plenty of small boys and rowdies who were ready to assail them with taunts and oyster-shells. Not until a snowy night in March 1770,

A VIEW OF PART OF THE TOWN OF BOSTON IN NEW ENGLAND AND BRITTISH SHIPS OF WAR LANDING THEIR TROOPS. 1768

however, did the inevitable head-on collision take place. By that time Bernard had gone back to England and Thomas Hutchinson was doing his conservative best as Acting-Governor. There had already been trouble in the daytime and the crowd that taunted the lone sentry before the Customs House that night may have been assembled by deliberate design. By hook or by crook Samuel Adams and the more rabid local patriots were determined to oust the hated red-coats.

At all events, the harassed sentry called for help and Captain Preston with seven more red-coats came to his rescue. The Captain bore a 'good character,' but some of the relief—especially a man named Kilroy—did not. In the

The 29th Regiment have already left us, and the 14th Regiment are following them, so that we expect the Town will soon be clear of all the Troops. The Wisdom and true Policy of his Majesty's Council and Col. Dalrymple the Commander appear in this Measure. Two Regiments in the midst of this populous City ; and the Inhabitants justly incensed : Those of the neighbouring Towns actually under Arms upon the first Report of the Massacre, and the Signal only wanting to bring in a few Hours to the Gates of this City many Thousands of our brave Brethren in the Country, deeply affected with our Distresses, and to whom we are greatly obliged on this Occasion—No one knows where this would have ended, and what important Consequences even to the whole British Empire might have followed, which our Moderation & Loyalty upon so trying an Occasion, and our Faith in the Commander's Assurances have happily prevented.

Last Thursday, agreeable to a general Request of the Inhabitants, and by the Consent of Parents and Friends, were carried to their Grave in Succession, the Bodies of *Samuel Gray*, *Samuel Maverick*, *James Caldwell*, and *Crispus Attucks*, the unhappy Victims who fell in the bloody Massacre of the Monday Evening preceeding !

On this Occasion most of the Shops in Town were shut, all the Bells were ordered to toll a solemn Peal, as were also those in the neighboring Towns of Charlestown Roxbury, &c. The Procession began to move between the Hours of 4 and 5 in the Afternoon ; two of the unfortunate Sufferers, viz. Mess. *James Caldwell* and *Crispus Attucks*, who were Strangers, borne from Faneuil-Hall, attended by a numerous Train of Persons of all Ranks ; and the other two, viz. Mr. *Samuel Gray*, from the House of Mr. Benjamin Gray, (his Brother) on the North-side the Exchange, and Mr. *Maverick*, from the House of his distressed Mother Mrs. *Mary Maverick*, in Union-Street, each followed by their respective Relations and Friends : The several Hearses forming a Junction in King-Street, the Theatre of that inhuman Tragedy ! proceeded from thence thro' the Main-Street, lengthened by an immense Concourse of People, so numerous as to be obliged to follow in Ranks of six, and brought up by a long Train of Carriages belonging to the principal Gentry of the Town. The Bodies were deposited in one Vault in the middle Burying-ground : The aggravated Circumstances of their Death, the Distress and Sorrow visible in every Countenance, together with the peculiar Solemnity with which the whole Funeral was conducted, surpass Description.

24

confusion, and apparently without any orders, the soldiers fired on the crowd, killing or mortally wounding five persons. Hutchinson calmed the outraged citizenry by promising that justice would be done and in due course the Captain and eight men were tried for murder. The trial itself provided a notable example of Anglo-American justice. At the grave risk of loss of public standing, John Adams and Josiah Quincy defended the accused men, procuring the acquittal of all but two of them, who were convicted of manslaughter and branded on the hand. The authentic records which remain show that the crowd was quite as much to blame as the soldiers, and that there were ruffians on both sides in this fracas.

Such, however, was not the impression given by Paul Revere's famous engraving, which was put up for sale soon thereafter. This served the purposes of propaganda rather than the cause of historic justice, and to hundreds of colonial Americans who pinned it up in their kitchens it served as a constant reminder of British tyranny. The episode was grossly exaggerated, but no just man could deny that this little army of occupation was an intolerable affront to a liberty-loving people. Governor Hutchinson himself must have realized this in part, for he withdrew the hated regulars to an island in the harbor. If the British Empire had to be held together by bayonets, it was not the sort of empire to which the citizens of Massachusetts, who cherished the rights and privileges and immunities of freeborn Englishmen, could have been expected to adhere.

The fifth victim referred to in the text died after the publication of the story.

When redcoats fired on an unruly crowd in Boston's King Street it was called a 'bloody massacre.'

Under cover of darkness Captain Abraham Whipple led a flotilla of eight longboats from Providence in an attack on the British revenue cruiser Gaspee, which had been lured aground in Narragansett Bay.

MINOR FLURRIES BETWEEN STORMS

FOR SEVERAL YEARS the controversy between the colonial patriots and the mother country was quiescent. There was, however, the incident of the schooner *Gaspee*, a British customs vessel, which ran aground below Providence on a June afternoon in 1772 and was burned by Americans. Meanwhile in Massachusetts Bay Samuel Adams did not at all relax his vigilance in keeping the spark of discontent alive. His most constructive service to the colonial cause during this period of relative calm was the creation of a standing committee of correspondence by the Town of Boston and his call on the other Massachusetts towns to do likewise. Early in 1773 the Virginia House of Burgesses, under the leadership of Patrick Henry, Richard Henry Lee, Thomas Jefferson, and other bold spirits, created a provincial committee for intercolonial correspondence. Thus the patriots set up the machinery for communication and joint action.

Also, there was the famous episode of the Hutchinson Letters, in which Benjamin Franklin, the agent in England for Massachusetts and several other colonies, was much involved. These letters—six in number and presumably addressed to a British official—were shown to the eminent Dr. Franklin in England, and he received permission to send them to the Speaker of the Massachusetts House of Representatives, expecting that they would be passed around but neither copied nor printed. Sam Adams

The Gaspee's commanding officer was wounded and the vessel burned by the Rhode Islanders. It has been called the first overt act of war in the American Revolution.

read them to a secret session of the House and ultimately, with Hutchinson's knowledge, they were printed. The letters left no doubt of Hutchinson's opposition to the more radical patriots but actually revealed nothing about the Governor's attitude that was not already known. They greatly injured his popularity, nevertheless, and were followed by a petition to England for his removal. Franklin attended a hearing of the Privy Council on this petition and a highly dramatic scene ensued. The learned and already venerable Franklin—he was then sixty-eight—was violently attacked by Attorney General Wedderburn as a common thief. He was forthwith removed from his office as Deputy Postmaster General for America. Before this time, though he did not know it, the Boston Tea Party had occurred, and this precipitated a major crisis.

Letters of Governor Thomas Hutchinson, 'Born and Educated among Us,' were publicized for propaganda purposes.

28

BENJAMIN FRANKLIN, *who was in London, was attacked as a common thief for having obtained the Hutchinson letters. His appearance before the Privy Council—depicted here by a nineteenth-century artist—concluded with his losing his job as Deputy Postmaster General for America.*

THE BOSTON TEA PARTY & WHAT CAME OF IT

THE BRITISH TEA ACT of May 10, 1773, was a measure of extreme unwisdom. It did not increase the tax that had been left on the statute books as a reminder of Parliamentary authority; on the contrary, by removing certain charges in England it permitted a lowering in the price of tea to the colonial consumer. But the measure was designed to help the powerful East India Company dispose of its vast tea surplus by giving it a virtual monopoly and permitting it to by-pass the colonial merchants. Thus, besides advertising anew a tax which was already a hated symbol, the Act united conservative and radical patriots—at just the time when in fact they were drifting apart.

There was objection in all the colonies, and many cases of tea were stored or sent back to England. The violence in Boston partly resulted from the stubbornness of the consignees, including close relatives of the Governor. The three tea ships that came to that harbor were unloaded on the night of December 16, 1773, but their cargoes went not into warehouses but into the water. Among the self-appointed stevedores disguised as Mohawks was Paul Revere, and if Sam Adams was not there he instigated the whole business. Disciplinary measures followed in the spring, in the Coercive, or Intolerable, Acts, which closed the port of Boston and sought to remodel the government of Massachusetts Bay. But, far from intimidating the colonials and isolating the Massachusetts culprits, these caused patriots from one end of the colonies to the other to rally in support of Boston. The spirited action in the harbor had been lawless beyond a doubt and was interpreted as an attack on property, but the Coercive Acts were sheer folly—against which Lord Chatham and Edmund Burke vainly protested. Colonists would not tamely submit to a punitive attack on their economic life and their time-honored political institutions.

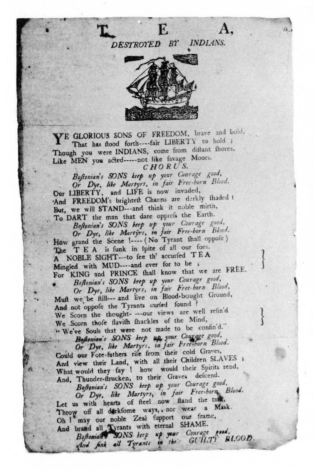

The British statesman Edmund Burke was one of the colonists' best friends in London, and he spoke eloquently in their behalf.

Sons of Liberty caught up with a Tory exciseman, tarred and feathered him, and forced scalding tea on him as a toast to the throne.

Paul Revere's engraving The Able Doctor, or America Swallowing the Bitter Draught is an almost exact copy of a cartoon published in the London Magazine, *April 1774.*

The situation in Boston, when the port was closed, was pictured by a contemporary London cartoon. The Bostonians were shown as colonial slaves, convicted of capital crimes, caged and left to starve. The gift of fish to the prisoners presumably alludes to codfish sent from Marblehead, one of many gifts to the distressed port.

The Tea-Tax-Tempest, or The Anglo-American Revolution. Time, with his magic lantern, presents an allegorical representation of the Revolution to Europe, Asia, and Africa. America sits at the left.

PATRIOTS
Take Counsel and Take Up Arms

A CONGRESS MEETS IN PHILADELPHIA, 1774

THE call for an intercolonial meeting to consider common grievances and means of redress came from several quarters, but the specific suggestion of place and date came from the House of Representatives of Massachusetts. Delegates were generally elected in an orderly manner, as became a people long accustomed to representative government; and upward of fifty of them, from all the colonies except remote Georgia, met in the early autumn of 1774 in Carpenter's Hall,

Philadelphia. The first Continental Congress, as this body has since been called, amounted to a convention of the Patriot party, though these were patriots of varying hues of radicalism and conservatism.

The Massachusetts delegation, including Samuel and John Adams, had made a triumphal procession to the scene, but, realizing that they might be regarded as extremists and that it was their colony which was seeking support, they wisely restrained themselves in the meeting. Peyton Randolph of Virginia, the large

34

*Carpenters Hall Phila in which the first
U S Congress sat in 1775*

Representatives of the aggrieved colonists came to Carpenter's Hall for the first Continental Congress.

and genial Speaker of the House of Burgesses, was unanimously elected President; and Charles Thomson, sometimes described as the Sam Adams of Philadelphia, was chosen as Secretary. This faithful man, who was active in the scientific circles of the American Philosophical Society (founded by Franklin) as well as in local politics, was destined to be the perennial Secretary of Congress until the Constitution of 1787 became effective. The delegates from Virginia seemed to John Adams the most spirited of them all. Among them were gaunt Richard Henry Lee, Patrick Henry—'the compleatest speaker'—and George Washington, who showed his spirit by appearing in uniform.

Thomas Jefferson, a younger man, was not in this Congress, but he had made known his

A

SUMMARY VIEW

OF THE

RIGHTS

OF

BRITISH AMERICA.

SET FORTH IN SOME

RESOLUTIONS

INTENDED FOR THE

INSPECTION

OF THE PRESENT

DELEGATES

OF THE

PEOPLE OF VIRGINIA.

NOW IN

CONVENTION.

BY A NATIVE, AND MEMBER OF THE HOUSE OF BURGESSES.
by Thomas Jefferson.

WILLIAMSBURG:

PRINTED BY CLEMENTINA RIND.

35

36

This London cartoon satirized the reluctance of many Virginia merchants to support the Continental Association, the purpose of which was to boycott British trade.

37

Determined women in Edenton, North Carolina, supported the Continental Association, said they would not drink tea or wear English-made clothing.

John Malcom, Tory tax collector, being tarred and feathered, Boston, January 20, 1775.

sentiments in the most important of his papers before the Declaration of Independence, *A Summary View of the Rights of British America,* which was written in the summer of 1774 and published that fall. In this pamphlet he assumed a constitutional position that was too advanced for this gathering, though not for John Adams, who was present, or for Benjamin Franklin, who was still in England. Agreeing with Charles Townshend that there was no valid distinction between external and internal taxes, he rejected both. Then he proceeded to assert that Parliament had no authority whatsoever over the colonies; he now recognized no constitutional tie with the mother country except that afforded by the person of the King. That is, he claimed

what was later known as Dominion status, while still avowing with everybody else his continued loyalty to the Crown.

This Congress was not ready to repudiate all parliamentary control, and nobody was yet urging independence. But the Congress did condemn the Coercive Acts as unconstitutional and tyrannical, along with a dozen others since 1763, thus countenancing the resistance of Massachusetts to them; it approved the arming of local militia and other defense measures; and it adopted the famous Continental Association, which was a non-importation, non-exportation, non-consumption agreement aimed at British trade. Enforcement was left in local hands, and the various local committees of ardent patriots

'*The Patriotick Barber of New York*' *honors Jacob Vredenburgh, who, in 1774, when half through shaving a British naval captain, learned his identity and refused to finish the job.*

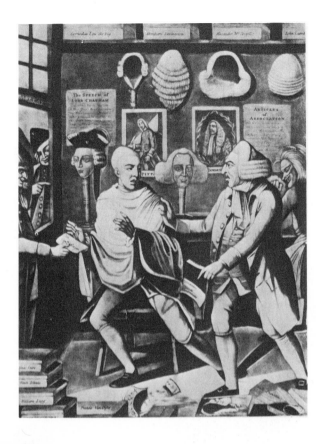

The resistance of Massachusetts to the Boston Port Act (the first of the Intolerable Acts, March 31, 1774), which ordered the port of Boston closed until restitution was made for the tea destroyed during the Boston Tea Party, is suggested in this September 1774 mezzotint. The fallen rider probably represents Major General Thomas Gage, the unpopular Governor of Massachusetts.

Give me LIBERTY OR Give me DEATH !

Patrick Henry.

did their duty well. Not everybody rose to the heights of self-denial that these regulations called for, but the Association was adopted by nearly all the colonies, and it imposed upon American daily life a degree of control such as was never equaled, perhaps, until our own time.

After a session of about seven weeks, Congress adjourned, having resolved to meet again in the spring if there had been no redress of grievances. Before that time Lord North made and Parliament approved a conciliatory proposal that was too little and too late. Hostilities had broken out before it could be considered; and in the meantime Massachusetts had been declared in a state of rebellion. In those days of slow communication, local events were inde-

pendent of contemporary actions on the far-distant parliamentary scene, and the train was already laid for violent explosion in Massachusetts. General Gage was now in command of the British troops in Boston, whence they marched into the countryside from time to time, seeking to forestall the militiamen in the collection of ammunition.

The clash of resounding arms had not yet been heard to the northward when a Virginia convention met in Old Saint John's Church in Richmond in March 1775, but Patrick Henry believed that war was inevitable unless the colonists should become abject. It was then, while urging greater military preparations on the part of his own colony, that he spoke his most

In Old Saint John's Church, Richmond, Henry urged a revolutionary convention to be more forceful. It was here that he said, 'Give me liberty, or . . . death.'

famous words: 'Give me liberty, or give me death.' Richard Henry Lee supported him eloquently; Thomas Jefferson, who as a rule avoided speechmaking, argued warmly on the same side; and certain of the Virginia militiamen afterward printed 'Liberty or Death' on their hunting shirts. These men were not yet demanding political independence from the King and Empire, but they were advocating resistance to what they regarded as tyranny and the defense of liberties which had been long enjoyed.

GENERAL THOMAS GAGE *commanded His Majesty's troops in troublesome Boston.*

THE CLASH OF RESOUNDING ARMS

THE STORY of events at Lexington and Concord on April 19, 1775, when the embattled farmers fired the shot that was heard round the world, has become part of the sacred folklore of the entire American people. The purpose of the British expedition was to destroy the supply of arms and ammunition at Concord and, if possible, to capture the Patriot leaders, Sam Adams and John Hancock, who were in Lexington. The silversmith Paul Revere and William Dawes, who were sent to spread the alarm, got to Lexington but were stopped before they reached Concord. Dr. Samuel Prescott gave the warning there and the British found few stores. At Lexington the relatively large detachment of British redcoats found a small body of minutemen drawn up on the village common, and in a moment of excitement fired on them without command, killing or wounding almost a score. There were practically no British casualties here, but there were a few at Concord Bridge and many more on the

way back. The total British casualties were nearly 300, while the American were less than a hundred. The King's men had been the aggressors, but the foray fared them ill.

In faraway Virginia, Jefferson noted that a 'phrensy of revenge' had seized upon all ranks of the people. More immediately, the provincial congress of Massachusetts authorized the raising of a large force and made appeals for aid which were quickly responded to by her neighbors. Within less than a month the second Con-

tinental Congress met, and in the middle of June it elected George Washington commander-in-chief of the Continental forces. The original suggestion came from John Adams, and the naming of this Virginian made the struggle a continental rather than a local conflict. Also, as we now know, Washington gave the colonial cause a nobility of spirit which it never lost. The battle of Bunker Hill, however, occurred on June 17, before he had arrived at Cambridge to take command.

43

PAUL REVERE'S *midnight ride ended with his capture by the British.*
They released Revere and three other prisoners early the next morning.

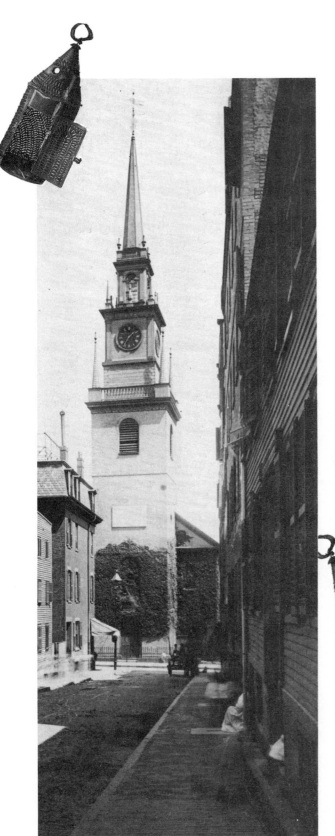

William Dawes *rode to Lexington by a different route, met Revere there and started to Concord with him. Dawes escaped capture and galloped back to Lexington.*

Paul Revere arranged with Charlestown friends that lights in the steeple of North (Christ) Church in Boston would signal the redcoats' route should they send an expedition to Concord.

At Lexington the British column encountered about seventy minutemen. Excited redcoats fired on them, and minutemen were killed, including their captain, Jonas Parker. A few minutes before he had said: 'Stand your ground. Don't fire unless fired upon. But if they want to have a war, let it begin here.'

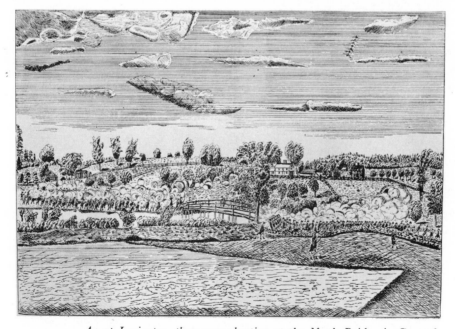

As at Lexington, there was shooting at the North Bridge in Concord. Minutemen and redcoats were killed. A small amount of American supplies was destroyed or damaged. Then the British column started back for Boston, and was harassed for sixteen miles by Americans attacking from cover.

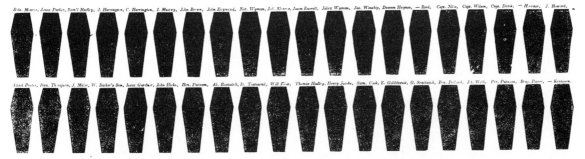

BLOODY BUTCHERY,

BY THE

BRITISH TROOPS:

OR THE

RUNAWAY FIGHT OF THE REGULARS.

Being the **PARTICULARS** of the **VICTORIOUS BATTLE** fought at and near **CONCORD**, situated Twenty Miles from Boston, in the Province of the Massachusetts-Bay, between Two Thousand Regular Troops, belonging to His Britannic Majesty, and a few Hundred Provincial Troops, belonging to the Province of Massachusetts-Bay, which lasted from sunrise until sunset, on the 19th of April, 1775, when it was decided greatly in favor of the latter. These particulars are published in this cheap form, at the request of the friends of the deceased **WORTHIES**, who died gloriously fighting in the CAUSE of LIBERTY and their COUNTRY, and it is their sincere desire that every Householder in the country, who are sincere well-wishers to America, may be possessed of the same, either to frame and glass, or otherwise to preserve in their houses, not only as a Token of Gratitude to the memory of the Deceased Forty Persons, but as a perpetual memorial of that important event, on which, perhaps, may depend the future Freedom and Greatness of the Commonwealth of America. To which is annexed a Funeral Elegy on those who were slain in the Battle.

The battle called Bunker Hill was on Charlestown peninsula, north of Boston. The Americans, seeking to forestall the British from occupying Dorchester Heights, were driven from Breed's Hill and then from Bunker Hill, and the British gained a nominal victory at an excessive cost. The colonists fought better for their liberties than they ever had for their King. Their casualties were much smaller than the British, but these included Dr. Joseph Warren, a major figure among the Boston Patriots who had just been voted a major-general's commission by the Massachusetts provincial congress. He had not yet assumed it, however, and met his death while participating as a volunteer. John Trumbull depicted the scene in one of the earliest of his historical paintings of the Revolution.

The list of the war's casualties had begun.

47

GEORGE WASHINGTON *of Virginia was elected commander-in-chief by the sec-*
ond Continental Congress, which convened as a result of events in Massachusetts.

*John Trumbull's painting of Bunker Hill was finished eleven years after
the battle. Though criticized for inaccuracy it is still a popular painting.*

First great battle of the war was
Bunker Hill. Of the attacking British,
1054 were killed or wounded. The
Americans suffered 371 killed or wounded according to one estimate, 411 according to another, and 30 were captured.

49

Benjamin Franklin was among those accredited to the second Continental Congress by Pennsylvania.

FIGHTING WITH WORDS, 1775

THUS THE COLONISTS took up arms in the spring of 1775, and their reasons for so doing were stated for them by the second Continental Congress in the summer. This body had met in Philadelphia in May, but it sat in the State House now rather than in Carpenter's Hall. There were important new members, including Benjamin Franklin, who was back from England and a member of the Pennsylvania delegation. This Congress, at the beginning, had the same President and Secretary as the first one, but after a couple of weeks John Hancock of Massachusetts succeeded Peyton Randolph of Virginia in the chair. Randolph returned to Williamsburg to preside over the House of Burgesses, which had been called into session by the irascible Governor, Lord Dun-

more. Randolph seemed to be more needed there, especially since so many of the leading Whig characters had gone to the Congress in Philadelphia—including Patrick Henry, whom Lord Dunmore regarded as a man of 'desperate circumstances' and had declared an outlaw. To fill Randolph's place as a delegate came Thomas Jefferson from the House of Burgesses.

This was the first time that this tall, sandy-haired, and studious Virginian had ever left his province on a public mission. He said afterward that he was drawn into public affairs against his personal tastes and wishes 'by emergencies which threatened our country with slavery, but ended by establishing it free.' He was destined to play a more important part in

When choleric Lord John Murray Dunmore, Governor of Virginia, called the House of Burgesses into session, Peyton Randolph came home from the Continental Congress to preside. Thomas Jefferson replaced him in Philadelphia.

establishing that freedom than he could have realized, and at a personal cost much greater than he could have expected. With two servants and four horses he made the ten-day trip from Williamsburg in more style than he could afford when he became President of the Republic more than a score of years later.

Though a fine gentleman he was not a pretentious person, and, having no flair for public speaking, he was a silent member during debate. On the other hand, he had a distinct flair for paper work and the reputation of his 'masterly pen' had preceded him. Not unnaturally, therefore, he was added to the committee for drawing A Declaration on the Necessity of

Taking Up Arms—along with the more cautious John Dickinson of Pennsylvania. He drew rather too strong a draft and the one that was adopted was mostly Dickinson's, though it retained some words of Jefferson's which set the controversy on a higher plane than that of mere taxation. Among other memorable things he said:

Our forefathers, inhabitants of the island of Great Britain, left their native land to seek on these shores a residence for civil and religious freedom.

Dickinson, who thought more in terms of the immediate questions at issue and was more hopeful of conciliation than Jefferson or John

51

JOHN DICKINSON *was the chief author of the 'Declaration on the Necessity of Taking Up Arms' adopted by Congress.*

Adams, also drew what is known as the Olive Branch Petition, but they all learned some months later that the King had not even deigned to receive it. Meanwhile, the Congress rejected Lord North's conciliatory proposal, which had finally arrived and come up for consideration. The crux of the proposal was that Parliament would *forebear* to tax any colony if it would make provision, to the satisfaction of Parliament, for its own expenses and government.

LORD NORTH'S *conciliatory tax proposal was rejected by the Congress.*

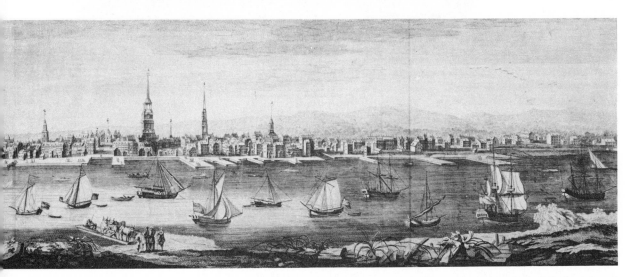

Philadelphia as members of the Congress saw it must have looked much as it does in this 'East Prospect . . . from the Jersey Shore' published in 1768.

This was wholly unsatisfactory to Jefferson, who drew the reply for Congress, 'because it imports only a suspension of the mode, not a renunciation of the pretended right to tax us.'

The liberty-loving Jefferson was convinced by now that arms would have to come to the support of words, and these various petitions and addresses seemed to John Adams little more than children's play at marbles or pushpin. Their chief contemporary value was in giving popularity to the Patriot cause; they were a phase of what we now call 'psychological warfare,' which the Patriots waged skillfully while the arrogant British officials of the era strengthened American opposition by their attitude of contempt. Chief of these arrogant Britishers was King George III, to whom the colonists were still professing loyalty. During the summer, when Congress was adjourned, the King proclaimed the colonies in open rebellion. By this time the differences between them and the mother country may have become

irreconcilable, but no one was more to blame than George III for the fact that no real alternative was left between open rebellion and complete submission.

When Congress reassembled in the autumn of 1775, the main body of opinion had caught up with Franklin, Jefferson, and John Adams, and the delegates were ready to deny their allegiance to Parliament. They did this in their reply to the royal proclamation that they were in rebellion. They still acknowledged the King, but to many it now seemed that he was the bitterest enemy of colonial rights and privileges. Force had been applied and had been met with resistance; and to many, though not yet to most, the inevitable next step seemed 'secession' from the Empire. Jefferson described the state of opinion in a letter to a British friend: 'We want neither inducement nor power to declare and assert a separation. It is will, alone, that is wanting, and that is growing apace under the fostering hand of our King.'

THE TORRENT
of
Independence

A MATTER OF COMMON SENSE

UBLIC opinion in favor of political independence developed rapidly in the early months of 1776. External events—such as the bellicose actions of Lord Dunmore, the Royal Governor of Virginia—were a strong contributing factor. This dour Scottish Lord, who had taken refuge on a British warship, had summoned the Negro slaves to revolt and join the King's forces, and at the very beginning of the New Year had caused the port of Norfolk to be bombarded. He was commonly blamed for the fire that followed and, though not mentioned by name, he directly inspired a denunciatory sentence that Jefferson afterward put into the Declaration. Dunmore had 'ravaged our coasts,' and there were other threats to the southward, but in March the British evacuated Boston, and after the temporary withdrawal of the regulars to Halifax they had no foothold in the colonies until late summer. Also, as the spring wore on, the Patriot leaders had intimations of likely aid from the French against their old enemy.

The military and diplomatic situation had become more encouraging but the most important influence upon the public mind was exerted by a pamphlet of forty-seven pages called *Common Sense*. Published in January and sold for two shillings, it attained a reputed sale of 120,000 in the first three months, and some half a million copies appear to have been sold altogether. In view of the small population of the country at the time, these figures were phenomenal. This brief work still commands great interest, for there is timelessness in its nervous and vivid prose, while there is universality in its spirit.

The author, Thomas Paine, thirty-nine years old, had come to America from England a few years before, bearing letters of introduction from Benjamin Franklin, who was then serving as colonial agent in London. Defeated, like many another, in the battle at home, Paine had sought to avail himself of the opportunities of a new world, occupying himself as a journalist. According to the custom of the time, however, he published this pamphlet anonymously; and in the preface to the third edition he said that knowledge of the Author was wholly unnecessary to the public, since the proper object of attention was 'the *Doctrine itself,* not *the Man.*' The pamphlet was so much in the spirit of Benjamin Franklin that many attributed it to that famous newspaper man, who alone among the leading Patriots could have matched the brisk journalistic style. Paine had consulted Dr. Benjamin Rush of Philadelphia about it, but in its freedom from inhibitions and its revolutionary fervor the work was distinctively his own. He served more cautious minds as a catalytic agent, and the American Patriots roundly applauded him when they determined his identity. It is an idle question just how soon this was, for the really important thing was *what* was said, not *who* said it. The comment of George Washington was indicative of patriotic opinion: the sober General thoroughly approved this 'sound doctrine and unanswerable reasoning.'

The chief significance of this burning pamphlet lay in its call for immediate independence. Paine skillfully marshaled practical arguments

but, like most agitators, he minimized difficulties for which responsible leaders had to allow. In dealing with the constitutional controversy he may have made no points not already made by James Otis, John Adams, Thomas Jefferson, and others; but he went beyond the specific questions at issue to make a powerful attack on monarchy as an institution, the British monarchy in particular, and to set forth in glowing language the virtues of a republic. He asserted that 'a thirst for absolute power is the natural disease of monarchy.' Also, he said: 'A government of our own is a natural right.'

His complete identification of himself with the colonial cause may have been presumptuous in such a recent comer, but no Patriot could object when he glorified and universalized it. 'The sun never shined on a cause more just,' he said. The cause of America, he declared, was that of all mankind. No one until then had so clearly perceived or so strikingly described the historic mission of America as the hope and asylum of free peoples.

O ye that love mankind! Ye that dare oppose not only the tyranny but the tyrant, stand forth! Every spot of the old world is overrun with oppression. Freedom hath been hunted round the globe. Asia and Africa have long expelled her. Europe regards her like a stranger, and England hath given her warning to depart. O receive the fugitive, and prepare in time an asylum for mankind.

Thomas Jefferson had not yet spoken such inspiring words, but he heard these in his native county, where he was lingering in the spring of 1776 because of his own illness and the death of his aged mother. He received from one of his friends in Philadelphia 'A present of 2/ worth of Common Sense,' and it seemed to him, as it had to Tom Paine, that the period of debate was over. He and most of his fellows were ready for decisive action when he got back to Congress in the middle of the month of May.

57

THOMAS PAINE'S *writings were one of the most influential forces in the Revolution.*

COMMON SENSE;

ADDRESSED TO THE

INHABITANTS

OF

AMERICA,

On the following interesting

SUBJECTS.

I. Of the Origin and Design of Government in general, with concise Remarks on the English Constitution.

II. Of Monarchy and Hereditary Succession.

III. Thoughts on the present State of American Affairs.

IV. Of the present Ability of America, with some miscellaneous Reflections.

Man knows no Master save creating HEAVEN,
Or those whom choice and common good ordain.

THOMSON.

PHILADELPHIA;

Printed, and Sold, by R. BELL, in Third-Street.

MDCCLXXVI.

Paine's clarion-like COMMON SENSE *was reputedly bought by 120,000 Americans in three months. It was absurd that an island should rule a continent, he said.*

THE VOICE OF THE PROVINCES

THE FIRST COLONY that specifically empowered its delegates to support 'Independency' was North Carolina by action of its Provincial Congress on April 12. These instructions were not communicated to the Continental Congress for several weeks, however, and in the meantime that body adopted on May 10 a resolution of John Adams urging the various colonies to form governments of their own. The preamble of this occasioned more heated debate than the resolution itself, since it called for the full exercise of local government and the suppression of all royal authority, and this was not passed until five days later. Certain delegates from the middle colonies objected and sentiment among them continued to be more uncertain than among the New Englanders, the Virginians, the North Carolinians, and the Georgians. Adams, who was prone to superlatives and premature congratulations, regarded this as 'the most important Resolution that ever was taken in America,' interpreting it as meaning independence. It called for local actions and, while waiting for a more formal statement on behalf of all the colonies, the impatient New Englander noted that every day by every post, 'Independence rolled in like a torrent.' The delegates were getting letters from their constituencies.

The strongest current flowed from the largest of the colonies, Virginia, where a historic convention was meeting in this month of May. Leading Patriots such as Peyton Randolph and Patrick Henry were there instead of in Philadelphia, and Jefferson deeply regretted that he could not be, for something important was sure to happen. The day after he got back to the seat of Congress, his countrymen in Williamsburg adopted a resolution that not only authorized their representatives in Philadelphia to vote for and sign a declaration that the colonies

were free and independent states but also instructed them to propose that Congress make one. Coupled with these instructions were references to foreign alliances and a confederation. This provincial resolution, along with the earlier one from North Carolina, was presented on May 27 to Congress, where it lay on the table for ten days while the delegates debated other matters. Then on June 7 Richard Henry Lee, changing the wording somewhat, presented a resolution that embodied three explicit propositions:

That these United Colonies are, and of right ought to be, free and independent States, that they are absolved from all allegiance to the British Crown, and that all political connection between them and the State of Great Britain is, and ought to be, totally dissolved.

That it is expedient forthwith to take the most effectual measures for forming foreign Alliances.

That a plan of confederation be prepared and transmitted to the respective Colonies for their consideration and approbation.

The aristocratic Lee had long been one of the most active of the Patriot leaders, both at home and in Congress, and in eloquence he was rated only a little below Patrick Henry. He spoke here not for himself alone but for the Virginia delegation, of which he was the ranking member; that is, he had received a larger vote than any of the others in the provincial convention of the previous summer which had elected him, Jefferson standing next. The motion was seconded by John Adams, and the working alliance between Massachusetts and Virginia was thus cemented afresh. In the debate he and Lee were also the leading supporters of the resolution, along with George Wythe, the legal luminary who taught so many budding lawyers in Williamsburg. His pupil

Jefferson, who was even more ardent but who loathed debating just as George Washington and Benjamin Franklin did, sat silent and kept the notes on which this story largely rests.

The chief opposition came from representatives of Pennsylvania, New York, and South Carolina. These provinces had not yet made up their minds. As Jefferson put it, they 'were not yet matured for falling from the parent stem,' though fast advancing to that degree of ripeness. Meetings were being held, or about to be held, in most of the middle colonies and there was good reason to wait until these had spoken. There was no doubt about the attitude of the majority, but it was supremely important to present a united front to the world; hence the delegates waited until they should achieve unanimity. They wisely postponed to July 1 a vote on the resolution of independence.

By that time the Province of Virginia had become a State by the adoption of a Constitution and the election of Patrick Henry as Governor. There was nothing on earth that Jefferson would have so liked to be as the author of that first Virginia Constitution, and actually he sent a draft for it, but another task fell to his active pen. Since there seemed little doubt of the eventual vote for independence, Congress named a committee to draw a proper paper against that time. This committee consisted of Jefferson, John Adams, Franklin, Roger Sherman of Connecticut, and Robert R. Livingston of New York. The paper was drafted by June 28, when the committee presented it; but before describing the evolution of this as a document we shall carry the congressional story to the point when the delegates began to discuss it on July 3.

60

Richard Henry Lee of Virginia offered a resolution in Congress, 'That these United Colonies are, and of right ought to be, free . . .' This is believed to be in Lee's hand.

THE GREAT DECISION

ON JULY 1, according to agreement, discussion of Lee's resolution of June 7 was resumed, and this lasted two days. To be precise, the Congress resolved itself into a committee of the whole for this purpose. John Hancock gave up the chair and Benjamin Harrison of Virginia, a large and portly man, assumed it. This committee of the whole reported back to the Congress, which alone could take formal action. All they did at the end of the first day was to ask leave to sit again on the morrow. They did not report their proceedings and these are not contained in the formal Journal. For our knowledge of these we are dependent therefore on the notes and recollections of the persons present—especially those of John Adams and Jefferson.

In the committee of the whole the resolution was carried by the vote of nine of the thirteen colonies, each of which voted as a unit according to the rule of the Congress, no matter how many delegates it had. Pennsylvania and South Carolina were in the negative; the two delegates from Delaware split the vote of that colony; and the New Yorkers, who expected authorization from home eventually but had not then received it, abstained. This was considerably less than the unanimity that seemed desirable, hence the deferment of decision to another day.

In the debates, John Dickinson of Pennsylvania opposed the resolution. According to Adams, he elaborated at great length and with great eloquence and politeness what he had

said many times previously. What he objected to was not so much the action as the timing. Adams himself saw no real point in any sort of debate, since all the arguments had been presented—not only in the Congress but also in pamphlets and newspapers and in discussions at every fireside. He assumed the task of presenting them again, in favor of the resolution, however, because nobody else seemed disposed to speak, and also because a fresh delegation had appeared from New Jersey and these men insisted that they must hear the argument. Adams claimed that he had made no special preparation, and although he wished on this important occasion that he had the talents and eloquence of the ancient classical orators he never pretended he did. Jefferson later said of this old colleague that he 'was not graceful nor eloquent, nor remarkably fluent, but he came out occasionally with a power of thought and expression that moved us from our seats.' It was in this connection that Jefferson termed Adams 'our Colossus on the floor,' and in this instance the Colossus indubitably impressed the Jerseymen. One of them, Richard Stockton, called him 'the Atlas of American independence.'

The South Carolinians had implied that they would give in the next day for the sake of unanimity, as they did. The adherence of that far-southern province raised the vote from nine to ten. On July 2, a majority of the delegates present from Pennsylvania were favorable, two of the opponents of the resolution having stayed

61

Caesar Rodney of Delaware rode eighty miles, night and day, to break a tie in his delegation and give Delaware's support to Lee's fateful motion for independence.

away, and the affirmative vote was thus increased to eleven. New York still abstained for the same reason as before, but little Delaware provided a dramatic episode which was favorable to the cause of independence. An absent delegate, Caesar Rodney, had been hastily summoned. Riding eighty miles by night and day through rain and thunder, he got there in time to break the tie in his delegation. So the committee of the whole could now recommend action to the Congress, and the vote in that body was unanimous for all the colonies that voted. The adherence of New York was con-

fidently expected. It was given on July 9 by a convention there and on July 15 word of this reached Congress.

It must not be assumed that the sentiment of the entire population of the thirteen states approached this degree of unanimity, or that the action of this Congress would be recognized as binding by all the citizenry throughout the land. The Loyalists, or Tories, would not bow to this authority unless forced to, yet this group comprised perhaps a third of the total population and included many of the more prosperous people, especially in the North. The presence

JOHN ADAMS *seconded the Virginian's resolution.*

CONGRESS VOTING INDEPENDENCE.

of many and influential Loyalists was one of the main reasons why the middle colonies had been reluctant to press the issue of independence. The Patriots, or Whigs, had assumed control and they knew that besides the King they had the Loyalists to contend with, and many indifferent people to win over. By resolving to strike for independence they were assuming a grave risk. John Adams, like an eighteenth-century Winston Churchill, foresaw 'the toil, and blood, and treasure' which this venture would surely cost, although he also saw through the gloom 'the rays of ravishing light and glory.'

The vote on July 2 marked the great decision from which there could be no turning back, and it is no wonder John Adams thought *that* date should be celebrated in future years. The *act* of severing the tie with the mother country was then agreed to, and the resolution then adopted was a declaration. The discussion of July 3 and 4 was about the form of the announcement that marked the birth of a nation. It was about a document that was ready and waiting, and to the story of this we now turn. To us the document, and not the fateful resolution, is *the* Declaration.

Resolved   That these united colonies are and of right
ought to be free and independant states;
that they are absolved from all allegiance
to the british crown and that all political
connection between them and the state of
great Britain is and ought to be totally
dissolved

Report &c July 2. 1776.
No 3 The resolution for
independancy
agreed to July 2. 1776

65

Lee's resolution became the Congress's 'Declaration.'

THE CHARTER

of a Free People

DRAFTING THE DOCUMENT

THE name of Jefferson came first on the committee chosen to draw the Declaration, and that of John Adams was second, because that was the order of the vote. This seeming sign of preference for the former is not primarily attributable to his fame at this juncture; at thirty-three he was the youngest of the five, except for Robert R. Livingston, and his reputation could not have been expected to equal that of Franklin and Adams. But the resolution of independence had been introduced in the name of Virginia and the proprieties called for the selection of a representative of that province, which was the largest of them all anyway. The natural person to elect, it seems, would have been Richard Henry Lee, and some currency has been given to the explanation that he was left off because of his unpopularity. A better explanation is that Lee desired and expected to go home shortly, and that Jefferson stood next to him in the delegation.

In any case, this was a lucky choice, for Lee, though much the better speaker of the two, was far inferior to Jefferson as a writer and a mind. Along with a record of unflinching patriotism, the younger man had brought with him to Philadelphia 'a reputation for literature, science, and a happy talent for composition'; and his contemporaries had already noted his 'peculiar felicity of expression.' Beside his graceful and luminous prose the formal writings of John Adams seem ponderous and dull. As a coiner of aphorisms Franklin was second to none, of course, and the learned Doctor was never boring; but, as has been said with a wit

To THOMAS JEFFERSON *fell the task of drafting the formal Declaration of Independence.*

which would have delighted him, he would probably have put a joke in the Declaration if it had been committed to him. The logic of circumstances pointed the finger of destiny at Jefferson, not merely as the ranking committeeman but also as the author of the first great charter of the Republic.

The reminiscences of Adams and Jefferson are not in full agreement about what went on within the committee, though the differences are actually unimportant. According to the former, the committee met and appointed him and Jefferson on a subcommittee. Then he presented to his reluctant colleague reasons why

If BENJAMIN FRANKLIN *had drafted the Declaration, it has been said, he would probably have put a joke in it.*

the latter should draft the document. We quote these in their more sprightly version:

Reason first—You are a Virginian, and a Virginian ought to appear at the head of this business. Reason second—I am obnoxious, suspected, and unpopular. You are very much otherwise. Reason third—You can write ten times better than I can.

Jefferson himself denied that there was any subcommittee and said that he was asked by the full committee to make the draft. Adams may have advanced arguments like these, nonetheless, and there appear to have been several meetings of the whole group, during which the general character and form of the document were discussed. Jefferson submitted his draft to Adams and Franklin in advance of the others, because he specially valued their judgment. Suggestions of theirs were written in, the document was accepted by the full committee, and it was presented to Congress seventeen days after this committee had been named.

Jefferson then had lodgings in the house of a young man named Graff, at the southwest corner of Market and Seventh Streets, Philadelphia. Few other houses had been built in the vicinity and he had been hoping to gain the benefit of 'a freely circulating air.' Jefferson, who was capricious in his spelling, wrote the name of his landlord as 'Graaf' and remembered him as a bricklayer. At any rate, he had a brick house, three stories high, along with a young wife and an infant son who was afterward told that he often sat on the great man's knee. The lodger had the whole of the second floor, consisting of a bedroom and parlor with stairs and a passageway between them. Jefferson wrote in the parlor, using a portable writing-box which has been preserved through the years, though Graff's brick house was torn down long ago.

Previously Jefferson had lodged with a cabinetmaker named Benjamin Randolph, who made this writing-box from the ingenious Virginian's own drawing. There is no reason to connect this cabinetmaker with the famous Virginia family of the name, with which the

GEORGE MASON *had served in 1759 with Washington in the Virginia House of Burgesses.*

author of the Declaration was so closely connected by blood and marriage, and in his extreme old age he spelled the name of his landlord 'Randall.' This was in the last year of his life, when he gave this writing-box to Joseph Coolidge, Jr., of Boston, husband of his favorite granddaughter, Ellen Randolph. 'It claims no merit of particular beauty,' he then said. 'It is plain, neat, convenient, and, taking no more room on the writing table than a moderate quarto volume, it yet displays itself sufficiently for any writing.' Even in 1776 he might have anticipated that this would become a precious heirloom, for the document he drafted on it was predestined to immortality.

We may assume that the parlor on the second floor of the Graff house was quiet and airy, but it contained no such library as Jefferson had left behind him at Monticello. Apparently he felt no need for one; he said afterward that he turned to neither book nor pamphlet while making his draft. He was not trying to compile a learned treatise, nor yet to create a work of the imagination, though he lavished on every word of this relatively brief composition the fastidious care of a poet and imparted to it the music that was in his soul. He was not straining for novelty, but, as he said later, was trying 'to place before mankind the common sense of the subject, in terms so firm and plain as to command their assent, and to justify ourselves in the independent stand we are compelled to take.' He intended this document to be 'an expression of the American mind,' and he sought to give it the tone and spirit that the occasion called for.

He said that it was not copied from any 'particular and previous writing,' but he must have had in mind at least one previous composition of his own. Before the middle of June he had put on paper his ideas about a desirable constitution for his native commonwealth, and had sent a draft to the convention in Williamsburg by his old friend and teacher George Wythe,

who was going home. The preamble of this consisted of a series of charges against George III—who had endeavored to pervert his kingly office into 'a detestable and insupportable tyranny.' Jefferson's proposed constitution was not accepted, partly because of its late submission, but his charges against the King were adopted as a preamble. The charges which comprise the larger part, though not now the best-known part, of the Declaration are very similar. Jefferson must have availed himself of his own earlier handiwork, but he now improved upon it.

In some sense the most famous part of the Declaration—the brief philosophical passage almost at the beginning—had also been recently anticipated. In advance of their constitution his fellow Virginians had adopted a Declaration of Rights, drawn by George Mason of Gunston Hall, in which the universal rights of human beings were proclaimed. This justly

Jefferson drafted the Declaration on a portable writing desk of his own design.

71

famous document had appeared in print in Philadelphia in time for Jefferson to see it. He undoubtedly liked it, for it said much the same thing that was in his own mind, but he no more needed to turn to it for arguments and language than he did to a book or pamphlet. He claimed no originality for the philosophy he embodied in the Declaration; it was an expression of the mind of the American patriots in his age and he was among the first of these.

Nobody knows exactly how long the work of composition took, but at some time before June 28 Jefferson copied what we now know as the 'Rough Draft' from an original which exists only in fragments. Before submitting this to the full committee of five he showed it to Adams and Franklin, presumably in that order because the latter was ill, and he immediately took advantage of certain of their suggestions. Adams made a copy for himself, and this has proved a great help to students in their effort to determine the times of the various alterations. The Rough Draft remains as the master copy, on which all later changes were marked, and it is a document of absorbing interest. Jefferson kept it all his life, and one man who looked at it at Monticello said it was 'scored and scratched like a school boy's exercise.' Some of the changes are labeled as those of Franklin or Adams; others, in the handwriting of Jefferson, may represent another's judgment or his own; still others, as we know, were made by Congress. Scholars have counted up more than four score altogether, though most of these are matters of verbal detail.

One of the most interesting of these (page 1) is the substitution of 'self-evident' truths for 'sacred and undeniable' truths. It will also be noticed that the word 'inalienable' appears in the text, though this has come down the years in printed versions as 'unalienable,' whether because of Congress or the printer. Also, Jefferson habitually used 'it's' in cases where we should omit the apostrophe, and this idiosyncracy did not appear. The most important cuts were made by Congress, especially in the omission of the perfervid passage about the slave trade (page 4). In view of the handling it had at the time and has had since, this priceless document is remarkably preserved and surprisingly legible. A fresh draft in Jefferson's hand was drawn for submission to Congress.

It seems that he fared well at the hands of his fellow committeemen. The record does not show what part Roger Sherman and Robert R. Livingston played in the emendation, and the changes suggested by Adams and Franklin were only minor. But the author was far less happy when his handiwork was subjected to what he called the 'depredations' of Congress. In his opinion, they did a good deal of damage in two days. When the Declaration became the order of business on July 3, following the adoption of the resolution of independence on July 2, the delegates took a hand in the drafting.

Adams supported the written document strongly upon the floor, just as was to be expected, but Jefferson kept silent for propriety's sake. Franklin had the same dislike for public disputation, and on the rare occasion when he made a speech it was a very short one. His prudence caused him even to avoid being the draftsman of papers subject to review by a public body—for reasons which he gave Jefferson in a story. He associated this with an old acquaintance of his, but it just as well could have come out of Aesop's Fables.

It was about a hatter who was opening a shop and wanted a handsome signboard, suitably inscribed. He started out with the following inscription, to which he added the figure of a hat: 'John Thompson, Hatter, makes and sells hats for ready money.' One of his friends thought 'hatter' superfluous, so that word went out. Another thought the word 'makes' unnecessary, since the purchasers of hats did not care who made them. A third thought the reference to 'ready money' superfluous, since nobody expected credit of him. All that was now left was 'John Thompson sells hats.' But another reminded him that nobody would expect him to give them away. All that was left, finally, was the name 'John Thompson,' along with the picture of a hat painted on the board.

A Declaration by the Representatives of the UNITED STATES
OF AMERICA, in General Congress assembled.

When in the course of human events it becomes necessary for ~~a~~ one people to
dissolve the political bands which have connected them with another, and to as
-sume among the powers of the earth the ~~separate and equal~~ station to
which the laws of nature & of nature's god entitle them, a decent respect
to the opinions of mankind requires that they should declare the causes
which impel them to the ~~change~~ separation.

We hold these truths to be ~~self-evident~~, that all men are
created equal ~~& independent~~, that ~~from that equal creation they derive~~ they are endowed by their creator with
~~rights~~ inherent & inalienable, among ~~which~~ these are ~~the preservation of~~ rights; that
life, & liberty, & the pursuit of happiness; that to secure these ~~ends~~, go
-vernments are instituted among men, deriving their just powers from
the consent of the governed; that whenever any form of government
~~shall~~ becomes destructive of these ends, it is the right of the people to alter
or to abolish it, & to institute new government, laying it's foundation on
such principles & organising it's powers in such form, as to them shall
seem most likely to effect their safety & happiness. prudence indeed
will dictate that governments long established should not be ~~changed~~ for
light & transient causes: and accordingly all experience hath shewn that
mankind are more disposed to suffer while evils are sufferable, than to
right themselves by abolishing the forms to which they are accustomed. but
when a long train of abuses & usurpations [begun at a distinguished period
&] pursuing invariably the same object, evinces a design to ~~subject~~ reduce
them under absolute Despotism, it is their right, it is their duty, to throw off such
government & to provide new guards for their future security. such has
been the patient sufferance of these colonies; & such is now the necessity
which constrains them to expunge their former systems of government.
the history of the present King of Great Britain is a history of unremitting injuries and
usurpations, [among which appears no solitary fact ~~to contradict~~ to contra-
-dict the uniform tenor of the rest [but all have] in direct object the
establishment of an absolute tyranny over these states. to prove this let facts be
submitted to a candid world [for the truth of which we pledge a faith
yet unsullied by falsehood]

Jefferson's original four-page rough draft is still preserved.

he has refused his assent to laws the most wholesome and necessary for the pub-
  -lic good:

he has forbidden his governors to pass laws of immediate & pressing importance,
    unless suspended in their operation till his assent should be obtained;
    and when so suspended, he has utterly neglected ~~utterly~~ to attend to them.

he has refused to pass other laws for the accomodation of large districts of people
    unless those people would relinquish the right of representation in the legislature, a right
    inestimable to them, & formidable to ~~tyrants~~ ~~only~~.

  as dissolved Repre- ~~sentative houses repeatedly & continually~~

  ~~manly~~ firmness his invasions on the rights of the people:
  ~~dissolved~~, he has refused for a long ~~space of time~~ time after such dissolutions, to cause others to be elected;
  ~~whereby the~~ legislative powers, incapable of annihilation, have returned to
    the people at large for their exercise, the state remaining in the mean time
    exposed to all the dangers of invasion from without, & convulsions within:

has endeavored to prevent the population of these states; for that purpose
    obstructing the laws for naturalization of foreigners; refusing to pass others
    to encourage their migrations hither, & raising the conditions of new ap-
    -propriations of lands:

he has suffered the administration of justice totally to cease in some of these
    states refusing his assent to laws for establishing judiciary powers:

he has made [our] judges dependant on his will alone, for the tenure of their offices,
    the & payment
    and amount of their salaries:

he has erected a multitude of new offices [by a self-assumed power,] & sent hi-
    ther swarms of officers to harrass our people, & eat out their substance:

he has kept among us in times of peace, standing armies [& ships of war,] without the consent of our legislature

he has affected to render the military independent of, & superior to the civil power:

he has combined with others to subject us to a jurisdiction foreign to our constitu-
    tions and unacknoleged by our laws; giving his assent to their acts of pretended
    & legislation, for quartering large bodies of armed troops among us;

    for protecting them by a mock-trial from punishment for any murders
    which they should commit on the inhabitants of these states;

    for cutting off our trade with all parts of the world;

    for imposing taxes on us without our consent;

    for depriving us of the benefits of trial by jury in many cases;

    for transporting us beyond seas to be tried for pretended offences:
    for abolishing the free system of English laws in a neighboring province, establishing therein an arbitrary government
    and enlarging it's boundaries so as to render it at once an example & fit instrument for introducing the same absolute rule

+ mr. Adams

+ Dr. Franklin

74

 abolishing our most ~~important~~ valuable Laws

for taking away our charters & altering fundamentally the forms of our governments,

for suspending our own legislatures & declaring themselves invested with power to

legislate for us in all cases whatsoever:

he has abdicated government here, [withdrawing his governors, & declaring us out

of his allegiance & protection:]

he has plundered our seas, ravaged our coasts, burnt our towns & destroyed the

lives of our people:

he is at this time transporting large armies of foreign mercenaries to compleat

the works of death, desolation & tyranny already begun with circumstances

of cruelty & perfidy unworthy the head of a civilized nation:

he has endeavored to bring on the inhabitants of our frontiers the merciless Indian

savages, whose known rule of warfare is an undistinguished destruction of

all ages, sexes, & conditions [of existence:]

[he has incited treasonable insurrections of our fellow-citizens, with the

allurements of forfeiture & confiscation of our property:

he has waged cruel war against human nature itself, violating it's most sa-

-cred rights of life & liberty in the persons of a distant people who never of-

fended him, captivating & carrying them into slavery in another hemi-

-sphere, or to incur miserable death in their transportation thither. this

piratical warfare, the opprobrium of infidel powers, is the warfare of the

Christian king of Great Britain. determined to keep open a market

where MEN should be bought & sold he has prostituted his negative

for suppressing every legislative attempt to prohibit or to restrain this

execrable commerce: and that this assemblage of horrors might want no fact

of distinguished die, he is now exciting those very people to rise in arms

among us, and to purchase that liberty of which he has deprived them,

by murdering the people upon whom he also obtruded them. thus paying

off former crimes committed against the liberties of one people, with crimes

which he urges them to commit against the lives of another.]

in every stage of these oppressions we have petitioned for redress in the most humble

terms; our repeated petitions have been answered only by repeated injuries. a prince

whose character is thus marked by every act which may define a tyrant, is unfit

to be the ruler of a people who mean to be free. future ages will scarce believe

that the hardiness of one man, adventured within the short compass of twelve years

only to lay a foundation so broad & undisguised for tyranny over a people fostered & fixed in principles

of freedom.]

Nor have we been wanting in attentions to our British brethren. we have
warned them from time to time of attempts by their legislature to extend a juris-
-diction over [these our states] we have reminded them of the circumstances of
our emigration & settlement here, [no one of which could warrant so strange a
pretension: that these were effected at the expence of our own blood & treasure,
unassisted by the wealth or the strength of Great Britain: that in constituting
indeed our several forms of government, we had adopted one common king, thereby
laying a foundation for perpetual league & amity with them: but that submission to their

credited: and we appealed to their native justice & magnanimity, [as well as to the ties
of our common kindred to disavow these usurpations which were likely to interrupt
our correspondence & connection &.   they too have been deaf to the voice of justice &
of consanguinity, [& when occasions have been given them, by the regular course of
their laws, of removing from their councils the disturbers of our harmony, they
have by their free election re-established them in power. at this very time too they
are permitting their chief magistrate to send over not only soldiers of our common
blood, but Scotch & foreign mercenaries to invade & destroy us. these facts

these unfeeling brethren. we must endeavor to forget our former
love for them, and to hold them as we hold the rest of mankind, enemies in war,
in peace friends. we might have been a free & a great people together; but a communication of grandeur & of freedom it seems is below their dignity. be it so, since they
will have it: the road to happiness & to glory, is open to us too; we will tread it
apart from them, and acquiesce in the necessity which denounces our
eternal separation!

We therefore the representatives of the United States of America in General Congress assembled, do, in the name & by authority of the good people of these [states,]
reject & renounce all allegiance & subjection to the kings of Great Britain
& all others who may hereafter claim by, through, or under them; we utterly
dissolve & break off all political connection which may have heretofore sub-
-sisted between us & the people or parliament of Great Britain; and finally
we do assert and declare these colonies to be free and independant states,
and that as free & independant states they shall hereafter have full power to levy
war, conclude peace, contract alliances, establish commerce, & to do all other
acts and things which independant states may of right do. And for the
support of this declaration] we mutually pledge to each other our lives, our
fortunes, & our sacred honour.

This story may have brought some comfort to the writhing author, and Congress did not go so far as to eliminate everything but the resolution of independence, though the delegates, unlike some later congressmen, effected economy in words. Actually, they helped his composition more than they hurt it. They deleted unnecessary phrases at a number of places, and eliminated the most extravagantly worded of all the charges—the one about the foreign slave trade. This trade richly deserved condemnation, and the British government had certainly imposed obstacles when the province of Virginia had sought to stop it, but the inhumane traffic and its train of evils could not be so exclusively blamed on George III. The South Carolinians and Georgians were not ready to end it, and the New Englanders were not unaware of the lucrative share they had had in it. The Declaration became stronger and fairer when Jefferson's most eloquent passage was left out; this overstrained rhetoric would actually have weakened it. The Congress employed wise tactics when it deleted a passage in which Scottish mercenaries were coupled with foreign, for this would have offended Scots in America as well as in Scotland. A reference to 'foreign mercenaries' was left in another place, but could be interpreted as meaning the Hessians. Very properly, Congress changed Jefferson's final paragraph so as to include in it the precise language of the resolution of independence just adopted. It left out several moving phrases of his toward the end, unfortunately perhaps, but it did not alter his final words: 'we mutually pledge to each other our lives, our fortunes, and our sacred honour.'

The function that Congress had performed, wisely on the whole, was editorial. The author himself had breathed eternal life into what easily might have been a dull state paper, and had imparted to it not merely his own rare felicity of phrase but, what was more important, a noble elevation of spirit. The Declaration is no mere political manifesto. As has been well said, it is 'a kind of war-song; it is a stately and passionate chant of human freedom; it is a prose lyric of civil and military heroism.' Jefferson himself never described it in such glowing terms, and he thought of himself as a scientist, not a poet. But time healed the wounds inflicted on his spirit by the congressional editors, and his pride in the Declaration increased with the passing years, until at the last it stood first in his own mind among his memorable achievements. To his countrymen, also, it has seemed that the first public paper of the Republic is the best one. They might easily have wearied under endlessly repeated readings, but actually they never have. Its well-worn phrases still have the freshness of life because it nobly evokes the undying spirit of human freedom.

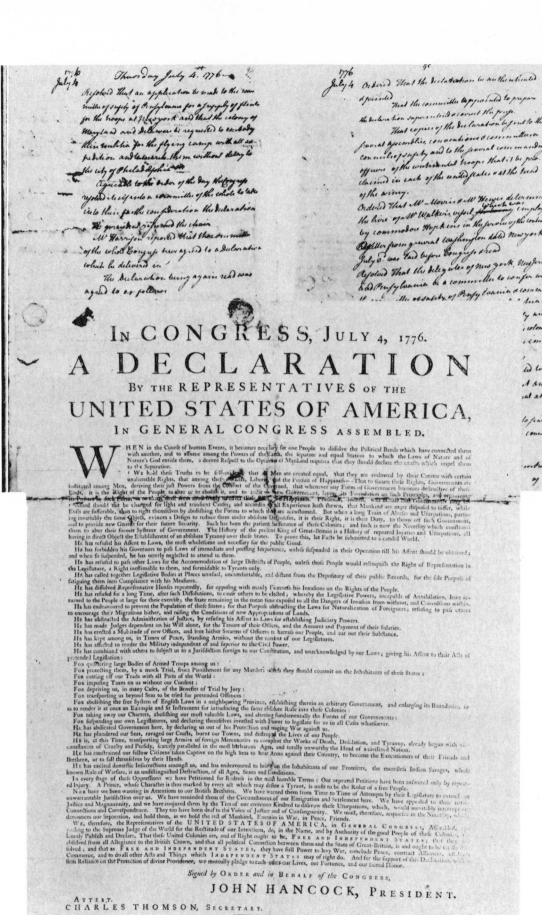

A copy of Dunlap's printing was wafered into the Rough Journal of Congress.

THE DECLARATION IS PROCLAIMED

CONGRESS ORDERED that the Declaration be authenticated, and on July 4th, President John Hancock and Secretary Charles Thomson signed it. The printing of the document was also ordered, and the committee of five was instructed to attend to this. If Jefferson saw it through the press, he permitted certain departures from the manuscript, which is preserved in his papers. It has been wittily said that the capitalization and punctuation followed 'neither previous copies, nor reason, nor the custom of any age known to man,' and the people who have bothered about the matter have generally blamed the first printer. The

CHARLES THOMSON, *as Secretary of the Congress, attested President John Hancock's signature on the Declaration.*

John Dunlap's printing shop was busy the night of July 4 printing the first official text of the Declaration.

copy (which has not survived) may have been hard to follow, and John Dunlap had to work fast. He printed the Declaration that night in a broadside that may be capricious in its punctuation and its capital letters but is very satisfying in its typography.

A blank space had been left for it in the Rough Journal of Congress, and on the next day it was attached there by a wafer. This printed version thus became the first official copy. Owing to the abstention of the New York delegates from the final vote, it could not yet be called the 'Unanimous Declaration' of the thirteen states. It was modestly entitled 'A Declaration by the Representatives of the United States in General Congress Assembled,' and it bore no names except those of Hancock and Thomson. In this congressional document there was naturally no acknowledgment to Jefferson and the committee.

Congress had ordered that copies of the Declaration be sent to the several assemblies and conventions, to the committees or councils of safety, and to the commanding officers of the continental troops in order that it might be proclaimed in every state and to the army. These copies began to go off on July 5th, but many of the broadsides were a long time reaching their destination. If horses ran any faster in 1776 than they did in the time of the Roman emperors the American roads were worse. The

first broadside was received by the Committee of Safety in Philadelphia, but several days were required to arrange a suitable celebration. The Declaration was proclaimed in its native city on July 8, as it was that day in Easton, Pennsylvania, and Trenton, New Jersey.

The proclamation in the yard of the State House of Pennsylvania is of special interest. One hostile observer said that 'very few respectable people' were present, and it certainly should not be supposed that enthusiasm was universal in the City of Brotherly Love. There were always many Loyalists among its more sedate and prosperous citizens, and probably few of that class were present. But John Adams reported that there was a great crowd of people —most of them plain, perhaps—and they left no doubt of their approbation. The Declaration was read—presumably by John Nixon, a member of the Committee of Safety—from what Adams described as 'that awfull stage.'

'The Manner in which the American Colonists Declared themselves Independent of the King.'

81

This was a circular platform that had been erected by the American Philosophical Society for astronomical observation, and from it David Rittenhouse often observed the stars and planets. The scientific setting was accidental, and Adams and Jefferson were not featured. Actually, they were not yet members of the American Philosophical Society, though their colleague Franklin was the founder. Jefferson must have been there though he did not mention it. There was great popular exultation. Cheers rose to the sky, the bells rang all day and almost all night, even the chimers of the eminently respectable and conservative Christ Church joining in, and despite the shortage of powder there were volleys from the militia.

Celebrations followed throughout the land, as the post riders proceeded with their printed copies of the Declaration. General Washington, who was then in New York, had the several brigades of the army drawn up at 6 p. m. on July 9 to hear it read. It was in this city on that very night that the leaden equestrian statue of

JOHN NIXON *had the honor of reading the Declaration on July 8, 1776, in Philadelphia.*

This contemporary French etching, one of a number of prints published both in Paris and in Germany, reveals the interest Europeans had in the events taking place in the colonies.

La Destruction de la statue royale à Nouvelle Yorck.

King George III was thrown down, and a literary gentleman compared the fallen monarch to Lucifer. The expectation, afterward largely fulfilled, was that the lead would be used for bullets 'to assimilate with the brain of our infatuated adversaries.' But General Washington, who stood to gain ammunition, did not like such rioting; he favored a decorous revolution.

In more distant Boston, on July 18th, Abigail Adams, after listening to a good sermon, followed the crowd that gathered before the State House and heard the Declaration proclaimed from the balcony. She also informed her husband John that the King's arms were afterward taken down and burned in King Street, along with other vestiges, thus ending royal authority in this state. The destruction of regal symbols went on in many places. A picture of the King was burned in Dover, Delaware, while the militia made a circle round the fire. Toward the end of July a child was baptized in East Windsor, Connecticut, by the name of 'Independence,' and before the middle of August the Declaration had arrived in remote Georgia, which was generally reached from Philadelphia by sail. It was read in Savannah at the Liberty Pole and at the Battery. Afterward the officials and other gentlemen dined and drank toasts under the trees, and that night George III was solemnly interred—that is, as the speaker of the occasion said, his 'political existence' was.

In all these celebrations emphasis was laid on what the former colonists were escaping from. The charter of the new Republic was read and applauded, and it may even have been heard if the clamor subsided sufficiently. It was also published in the newspapers throughout the land, and anyone who wanted to know what its contents and meaning really were would have done well to read it for himself in a calmer moment. This we can do with ease, for it has been reprinted countless times, and we have certain advantages in perspective.

Raising the liberty pole on a village green.

83

The Declaration of Independence

---

4 July 1776

THE UNANIMOUS DECLARATION OF THE THIRTEEN UNITED STATES OF AMERICA

-»»-»» * «-««

WHEN IN THE COURSE OF HUMAN EVENTS, it becomes necessary for one people to dissolve the political bands which have connected them with another, and to assume among the powers of the earth the separate and equal station to which the Laws of Nature and of Nature's God entitle them, a decent respect to the opinions of mankind requires that they should declare the causes which impel them to the separation.

WE HOLD THESE TRUTHS TO BE SELF-evident, that all men are created equal, that they are endowed by their Creator with certain unalienable rights, that among these are life, liberty, and the pursuit of happiness. That to secure these rights, governments are instituted among men, deriving their just powers from the consent of the governed. That whenever any form of government becomes destructive of these ends, it is the right of the people to alter or to abolish it, and to institute new government, laying its foundation on such principles and organizing its powers in such form, as to them shall seem most likely to effect their safety and happiness. Prudence, indeed, will dictate that governments long established should not be changed for light and transient causes; and accordingly all experience hath shown, that mankind are more disposed to suffer, while evils are sufferable, than to right themselves by abolishing the forms to which they are accustomed. But when a long train of abuses and usurpations, pursuing invariably the same object evinces a design to reduce them under absolute despotism, it is their right, it is their duty, to throw off such government, and to provide new guards

for their future security. Such has been the patient sufferance of these Colonies; and such is now the necessity which constrains them to alter their former systems of government. The history of the present King of Great Britain is a history of repeated injuries and usurpations, all having in direct object the establishment of an absolute tyranny over these States. To prove this, let facts be submitted to a candid world.

He has refused his assent to laws, the most wholesome and necessary for the public good.

He has forbidden his Governors to pass laws of immediate and pressing importance, unless suspended in their operation till his assent should be obtained; and when so suspended, he has utterly neglected to attend to them.

He has refused to pass other laws for the accommodation of large districts of people, unless those people would relinquish the right of representation in the legislature, a right inestimable to them and formidable to tyrants only.

He has called together legislative bodies at places unusual, uncomfortable, and distant from the depository of their public records, for the sole purpose of fatiguing them into compliance with his measures.

He has dissolved representative houses repeatedly, for opposing with manly firmness his invasions on the rights of the people.

He has refused for a long time, after such dissolutions, to cause others to be elected; whereby the legislative powers, incapable of annihilation, have returned to the people at large for their exercise; the State remaining in the meantime exposed to all the dangers of invasion from without and convulsions within.

He has endeavoured to prevent the population of these

States, for that purpose obstructing the laws for naturalization of foreigners; refusing to pass others to encourage their migration hither, and raising the conditions of new appropriations of lands.

He has obstructed the administration of justice, by refusing his assent to laws for establishing judiciary powers.

He has made judges dependent on his will alone, for the tenure of their offices, and the amount and payment of their salaries.

He has erected a multitude of new offices, and sent hither swarms of officers to harass our people, and eat out their substance.

He has kept among us, in times of peace, standing armies without the consent of our legislatures.

He has affected to render the military independent of and superior to the civil power.

He has combined with others to subject us to a jurisdiction foreign to our constitution, and unacknowledged by our laws; giving his assent to their acts of pretended legislation:

For quartering large bodies of armed troops among us:

For protecting them, by a mock trial, from punishment for any murders which they should commit on the inhabitants of these States:

For cutting off our trade with all parts of the world:

For imposing taxes on us without our consent:

For depriving us in many cases of the benefits of trial by jury:

For transporting us beyond seas to be tried for pretended offences:

For abolishing the free system of English laws in a neighbouring Province, establishing therein an arbitrary government, and enlarging its boundaries so as to render it at once an example and fit instrument for introducing the same absolute rule into these Colonies:

For taking away our Charters, abolishing our most valuable laws, and altering fundamentally the forms of our governments:

For suspending our own Legislatures, and declaring themselves invested with power to legislate for us in all cases whatsoever.

He has abdicated government here, by declaring us out of his protection and waging war against us.

He has plundered our seas, ravaged our coasts, burnt our towns, and destroyed the lives of our people.

He is at this time transporting large armies of foreign mercenaries to compleat the works of death, desolation, and tyranny, already begun with circumstances of cruelty and perfidy scarcely paralleled in the most barbarous ages, and totally unworthy the head of a civilized nation.

He has constrained our fellow citizens taken captive on the high seas to bear arms against their country, to become the executioners of their friends and brethren, or to fall themselves by their hands.

He has excited domestic insurrections amongst us, and has endeavoured to bring on the inhabitants of our frontiers the merciless Indian savages, whose known rule of warfare is an undistinguished destruction of all ages, sexes, and conditions.

In every stage of these oppressions we have petitioned for redress in the most humble terms: our repeated petitions have been answered only by repeated injury. A prince whose character is thus marked by every act which may define a tyrant, is unfit to be the ruler of a free people.

Nor have we been wanting in attention to our Brittish brethren. We have warned them from time to time of attempts by their Legislature to extend an unwarrantable jurisdiction over us. We have reminded them of the circumstances of our emigration and settlement here. We have appealed to their native justice and magnanimity, and we have conjured them by the ties of our common kindred to disavow these usurpations, which would inevitably interrupt our connections and correspondence. They too have been deaf to the voice of justice and of consanguinity. We must, therefore, acquiesce in the necessity, which denounces our separation, and hold them, as we hold the rest of mankind, enemies in war, in peace friends.

WE, THEREFORE, the Representatives of the United States of America, in General Congress assembled, appealing to the Supreme Judge of the world for the rectitude of our intentions, do, in the name, and by authority of the good people of these Colonies, solemnly publish and declare, That these United Colonies are, and of right ought to be Free and Independent States; that they are absolved from all allegiance to the British Crown, and that all political connection between them and the State of Great Britain is and ought to be totally dissolved; and that as Free and Independent States they have full power to levy war, conclude peace, contract alliances, establish commerce, and to do all other acts and things which independent States may of right do. And for the support of this declaration, with a firm reliance on the protection of Divine Providence, we mutually pledge to each other our lives, our fortunes and our sacred honor.

FACTS TO THE WORLD

THE PAPER that had been adopted by Congress and proclaimed from Georgia to New Hampshire can be roughly divided into four parts: a preamble, a philosophical paragraph, a list of charges against the King, and at the end the actual declaration of independence—including the resolution adopted on July 2. In the summer of 1776 greatest attention was paid to the last of these, for it represented the crucial decision and the fateful public act. Next in interest was the list of 'abuses and usurpations' justifying the severance of ancient political ties, and this was a center of attention in the mother country also.

In our times the emphasis is quite different. The resolution of independence marks the beginnings of the Republic, to be sure, but Americans have enjoyed political independence so long that they take it pretty much for granted. The continuing appeal of the Declaration lies in the opening sentences of the second paragraph, and the universal and timeless philosophy they express. Inseparable from them in most minds is the noble preamble, containing that matchless phrase, 'a decent respect to the opinions of mankind.' But the charges against the King, which comprise the largest section, can now be infused with reality only by the exercise of historical imagination. These specific grievances—these facts 'submitted to a candid world'—are no longer fresh in human memory. Happily, they have been forgotten by most Americans.

Congress went to particular pains to avoid the impression that it was indicting the British people, wisely toning down certain denunciatory expressions. Thus, while there is mention of vain appeals to the British public to disavow the 'usurpations' of American rights, the references to 'our British brethren' were made in a tone of sorrow rather than one of censure. As we have seen, the charges ignored Parliament, since the authority of that body had already been denied, but they did comprise a summary of colonial grievances over a considerable period of time, including legislative acts. These were the specific reasons for the cutting of the last tie with the mother country, and, while some of them were more generally understood than others, few of them needed to be explained. From the time of the Stamp Act everybody had known the meaning of 'imposing taxes on us without our consent.' From personal experience the citizens of Massachusetts had fullest comprehension of the reference to 'taking away our charters, abolishing our most valuable laws, and altering the frame of our governments,' but it was sufficiently understood elsewhere. The charges against the King were very real, and every one of them related to actual experience or potential threat.

They were stated baldly, to be sure, without regard for attendant circumstances and imperial problems. American historians of today, who have explored these matters with open minds and a zeal for truth, question whether these 'repeated injuries and usurpations' had as their direct object 'the establishment of an absolute tyranny over these states.' Some allowance must be made for the ignorance and stupidity of British officials, as well as for the obstreperousness of certain colonists. English historians have not often bothered to defend George III, who has remained the scapegoat, but he was not quite so sinister a figure as the one painted in the Declaration. As a despot he was not in a class with Stalin and Hitler, or certain other moderns who might be named.

Jefferson was using the language of political controversy, not of dispassionate scholarship. He was writing as an American partisan, making a case at the bar of public opinion. His personalizing of the grievances and concentrating on the King was not wholly warranted. But to

The engrossed Declaration was signed by members of Congress on August 2. Some signatures were added later.

his mind and the minds of the Patriots the issue had become clear and unescapable. British policy was threatening to destroy liberties that were dearer than life, and this policy was centered in the King, both as a symbol and a person. About this time the author of the Declaration got from his collaborator Benjamin Franklin a motto which he adopted for his own seal: 'Rebellion to tyrants is obedience to God.' Though never adopted officially, this was a fitting slogan for the American Revolution, and it was implicit in the Declaration.

TRUTHS TO HOLD

THE ABIDING SIGNIFICANCE of the document, as not merely the justification of a particular revolt of one people in specific circumstances, but as a perennial expression of human hope, lay in the few sentences that begin, 'We hold these truths to be self-evident.' The supreme merit of the author's achievement lay in the fact that he imparted a quality of timelessness and universality to what might have been merely a national document, and if his colleagues were not all fully aware of what he was doing, they did not object. Indeed, Congress made these 'truths' official American doctrine by adopting them at the beginning of the history of the Republic.

The meaning of this faith and doctrine may be somewhat obscured in our own day by terms which were thoroughly familiar at that time but which have become rather archaic. In that sense, and in that sense only, this part of the Declaration may seem dated. It harks back to the philosophy of natural rights which was better understood then than it is now. We doubt if there ever was a 'state of nature' in which all men were free; we are uncertain of the meaning of 'natural law'; we question whether human government was based in the first instance upon consent; and we slip over such an expression as 'unalienable rights' without fully comprehending what it implied in the eighteenth century.

Jefferson saw no need to define terms that the enlightened minds of his time understood, and we can get at the heart of the matter if we regard the word 'rights' as merely the plural of the word 'right' and think of it in the moral sense. Rights, as the people in all ages understand them, are simply what is right. Force does not make right and right derives from no king. Jefferson and his contemporaries found it in the universal law of nature; it arose from the nature of things. It came from God, and what God has given no man can take away; this is inalienable. 'Rights,' therefore, belong to all men because they are men and these rights last as long as life does. Jefferson expressed the same thought and voiced the same faith when he said: 'The God who gave us life gave us liberty at the same time; the hand of force may destroy, but cannot disjoin them.' Liberty is right and God intends that all men shall have it, and by the same token the force that tyrants use can never be anything but wrong.

It would be far too much to claim that this assertion of the freedom of the human spirit and the dignity of human nature was fully understood by everyone who threw up his hat when the Declaration was proclaimed, or that the implications of these 'truths' had been really faced by Congress. But many Americans must have sensed that they were doing far more than repudiating a king, that they were starting a Republic which had as its cornerstone the rights of free individuals, that here in a brave new world men would try to translate into human law and social institutions the laws of the moral universe. Beyond any doubt the author believed that the charter he drew had just that meaning.

SIGNING THE CHARTER

ONLY TWELVE STATES had voted for the Declaration on July 4, but the full number was soon rounded out. On July 19, soon after it received official notice of the action in New York, Congress resolved that the Declaration be engrossed on parchment with the title and style that have become so familiar:

'The Unanimous Declaration of the Thirteen United States of America.'

When engrossed, it was to be signed by every member of Congress. The copying on parchment was probably done by Timothy Matlack of Philadelphia, who had served for a time as assistant to Secretary Charles Thomson and was afterward a colonel in the Pennsylvania militia and a member of Congress. The copying was in the sort of writing customarily used in formal documents, which meant that it was easier to look at than to read; and the effort to get the title on one line led to results that were significant as well as amusing, since the word 'STATES' was written in large letters, while 'united' was in very small ones. This was not an inaccurate representation of the actual political situation. The engrossed Declaration was signed on August 2.

In those days Congress acted in no such glaring light of publicity as in our day, and official records were kept in no such detail as

TIMOTHY MATLACK *is said to have engrossed the formal Declaration on parchment for the members of Congress to sign.*

now. Hence for knowledge of events there has been necessary dependence on the records and memories of individuals, which are frequently in disagreement even among the best of men. Not unnaturally, therefore, controversy arose about the signing during the lifetime of the Signers, and there is some difference of opinion among scholars even now. Because of statements of Jefferson, who was an exceedingly careful man and kept good notes, it has been believed by some that there was a preliminary signing on July 4th—on a paper that has since disappeared. This would have been the report of the committee as emended by Congress, which was inevitably marked up, and it may possibly have been destroyed after August 2 for just this reason. The weight of learned opinion is against this earlier signing on paper, but the signing on parchment is open to no doubt.

By August some of the delegates who had voted on July 4 were not present to affix their signatures; new members had appeared and these did sign; and further signatures were added later. Thus the famous group of Signers who, in John Adams's phrase, transmitted their names 'among the Votaries of Independence,' was not identical with the group who had voted for the Declaration on the natal day of the Republic, and actually these Signers were never assembled as a group. Those who would dramatize these stirring events or depict these scenes find these divergences unfortunate and, of course, they often ignore them. Artists and dramatists can be confined within no rigid framework of chronology, whatever the factual historians and antiquarians may say.

To the lay public it is a matter of no great consequence, probably, that some of the Patriots in John Trumbull's deservedly famous

Legend has it that John Hancock said he would make his signature large enough for John Bull to read it without his glasses. His signature on the Declaration is about 4⅞ inches long, on a letter the same year about 3¾ inches.

'The Declaration of Independence.'

painting, 'The Declaration of Independence,' were not present on August 2, and that others of them were absent on July 4. It is a more important consideration that he painted three-fourths of these historic characters from life, even though he caught them later—as he did Jefferson some ten years afterward in Paris. Whether or not he depicted an actual scene on a specific day, he gave us Jefferson, Adams, Franklin, and the other committeemen, along with the President and Secretary of Congress and many others much as they must have looked in their own time.

The story of the signing has been embroidered with many colorful legends, and it would have been strange indeed if such had not been the case. The most engaging and one of the most familiar of these is associated with Franklin. According to this legend, President John Hancock observed: 'We must be unanimous; there must be no pulling different ways; we must all hang together.' Then Franklin replied: 'Yes, we must indeed all hang together, or most assuredly we shall all hang separately.' This saying appears to have got into print about half a century after Franklin's death, which was much too late for him to deny it, and as a witticism it certainly deserves to live.

Very likely there was contemporary talk of hanging, for under British law, which might very conceivably have been re-established, the Signers were all liable to the supreme penalty as traitors. Another story is told about Benjamin Harrison of Virginia, who carried much excess weight, and Elbridge Gerry of Massachusetts, who was slim and light. The former is reported to have boasted to the latter that he would have a much easier time when the moment for hanging came; his neck would be broken in an instant, while Gerry would be left kicking in the air for a half hour. This sally of wit could not have occurred on August 2, however, for Gerry was one of those who signed later.

Much better known is the story of John Hancock's signing. That he wrote his name in large bold letters anyone who looks at a reproduction of the historic document can see. He is supposed to have said that he did this so that John Bull could read it without spectacles, and could double the reward on his head. This was his famous 'defiance.' At all events, he created a figure of speech. From that day to this, 'John Hancock' has been a synonym for signature.

The name of Hancock, as President, had been attached to the Declaration that was first proclaimed, so there was no possible secret about his participation in these revolutionary events. Anybody who went to the trouble could have found the names of the other members of Congress, but these did not appear in print as Signers for some months yet. On January 18, 1777, Congress resolved that an authenticated copy of the Declaration, with the names of the members subscribing to it, be sent to each of the states. These were printed copies, though authenticated by the actual signature of Hancock which Thomson attested, and the printed names of the Signers were grouped by states. Even so, the list was incomplete, for the name of Thomas McKean of Delaware was left off. Presumably, he did not attach it till later and was the last of the Signers.

The Declaration on parchment, whose wanderings will be described in a later section, remained the official document. This appeared in 1823 in the copper-plate facsimile with which successive generations became familiar. On this the signatures and not just the names of the Signers appear—fifty-five altogether, in addition to Hancock. These were the historic 'Votaries of Independence.'

PART Two

THE SIGNERS

THE
Signers

ONE of the members of the Continental Congress in the summer of 1776, Dr. Benjamin Rush, said that when he entered that door, he considered himself 'a citizen of America.' Nevertheless, the fifty-five Signers of the Declaration of Independence besides the President attached their names in thirteen groups. Each delegation from a colony or state, regardless of its size, voted as a unit in the Congress in Philadelphia. The number of delegates varied; and, not unnaturally, more of them came from relatively populous Pennsylvania than from more distant and more sparsely settled New Hampshire and Georgia. The fact that there were more Signers from Pennsylvania than any other province or commonwealth does not indicate that revolutionary sentiment was strongest there. In reality it was sharply divided in the middle colonies and was probably strongest in Massachusetts and Virginia.

In age these men ranged from the twenty-six years of Edward Rutledge of South Carolina to Benjamin Franklin's seventy. They cannot be classified with precision on grounds of occupation, for this was not an age of specialization and occupations constantly overlapped. Lawyers were more numerous than the members of any other profession, but many of these were southern planters who got most of their living from the land rather than the law. There were four physicians, though their attention to medicine was far from exclusive; and there was one clergyman, John Witherspoon, president of the College at Princeton. The country was predominantly agricultural, but there were almost as many merchants as planters and farmers, and a couple of the Pennsylvanians might be described as manufacturers. Some delegates —notably Franklin and Jefferson among the major figures and Francis Hopkinson among the minor—defy classification because of the range and diversity of their interests and activities. At this stage practically all of them were devoting themselves to public affairs, though the class of professional politicians in the modern sense did not really exist.

But these men were entirely too well schooled in public affairs to be called amateurs and they took the road to revolution advisedly. Though bold in action they were not reckless adventurers, and with relatively few exceptions they were men of substance. By the standards of their time, a number of them were exceedingly wealthy. President John Hancock had fallen heir to a lordly fortune, and Robert Morris and Philip Livingston were merchant princes. Charles Carroll of Carrollton was reputed to be the richest man in the colonies, though among the great planters that title might be contested in behalf of General George Washington or Henry Middleton of South Carolina, whose son had succeeded him in Congress.

There were plain men among the Signers, as some of the portraits show unmistakably, and even though it may be true, as John Adams believed, that several 'signed with regret, and several others with many doubts,' they all stood forth in this instance as champions of liberty. But they were heralds of political self-government rather than class warfare and social rev-

olution, and it is an ironical fact that a very considerable number of them suffered grievously in their own fortunes in the course of the war. After signing their names, some of them soon drew into relative obscurity, leaving scarcely a trace behind. Most of them continued to render public service as long as they could, and some became major heroes of the young Republic. It is doubtful, however, if any of these men ever did anything that he took more pride in than signing the great Declaration. Certainly two of the most famous and longest-lived of them—John Adams and Thomas Jefferson—never did.

If the signatures on the engrossed document are read from left to right, one begins with Georgia and ends with New England—thus proceeding from south to north. In describing the men themselves, however, it seems better to proceed in the customary way from north to south, beginning in the part of the country where the revolt first broke out. The order of signatures within a delegation has no particular significance and need not be heeded. In certain cases in this book the arrangement of names follows the logic of events and circumstances, and as a general but not invariable rule age takes precedence over youth.

These 'votaries of independence' comprise a fascinating body of men by any reckoning. Greatest diversity was to be seen in the delegations of New Jersey and Pennsylvania, while those of New York and South Carolina and Maryland were probably the richest. The shortest-lived of the Signers was Thomas Lynch, Jr., of South Carolina, who affixed his name to the Declaration at twenty-seven and was lost at sea when thirty. The first to die was John Morton of Pennsylvania; Button Gwinnett of Georgia, who fell in a duel within a year, was a close second. The longest-lived was Charles Carroll of Carrollton who lived until 1832, dying at the age of ninety-five, in the beginning of the railroad era. None of the rest of them, apparently, ever saw anything faster than a horse.

The three Signers from New Hampshire had much in common besides their unflagging zeal for independence. All of them had been born outside of that province and had come there from the more populous colony of Massachusetts-Bay. Two of them were physicians and all three became judges, though no one of them was a lawyer. Their careers admirably illustrated the diversity of men's activities and the unspecialized nature of the professions in those days. Also, they show how patriotic citizens, in time of crisis, left whatever they were doing in order to perform larger public service.

JOSIAH BARTLETT.

JOSIAH BARTLETT, who is reputed to have cast the first vote for the Declaration, was in his forty-seventh year in the summer of 1776. Born in Amesbury, Essex County, in the province of Massachusetts-Bay, he had been living since the age of twenty-one at Kingston in southern New Hampshire, engaged in the practice of medicine but by no means confining himself to that occupation. Before the Revolution he served as a justice of the peace and provincial legislator and became a colonel of militia; after leaving the second Continental Congress he became a judge, and later still he was the chief executive of his state. In all these varied tasks he acquitted himself with ability and dignity. He is said to have been a tall man with a fine figure, to have worn his auburn hair in a queue, and to have been very particular about his dress—though the rather crude pencil drawing by John Trumbull does not bear out this description.

His staunch support of the cause of the Patriots led to his dismissal from the post of justice of the peace by the Royal Governor and, presumably, to the burning of his house. The latter event prevented his serving as delegate to the first Continental Congress, but he was reelected to the second and was present when the Declaration was adopted and signed. He served in later sessions, though not continuously, and he became increasingly critical of wordy debates, in which he rarely participated.

In 1779, when he was about fifty, he became chief justice of the New Hampshire court of common pleas, and he was afterward an associate justice and chief justice of the superior court. In the state convention he was one of the most effective advocates of the ratification of the United States Constitution, which is the more interesting because he is reputed to have cast the first vote in Congress for the Articles of Confederation which were to be superseded.

The ratification of the Constitution by New Hampshire was a notable event, because she was the ninth state and this assured the putting into effect of the new frame of government. For three successive years Bartlett was elected by large majorities as President of New Hampshire, and when the title was changed to Governor he was the first man to bear it (1793). The New Hampshire Medical Society was chartered during his administration (1791). He wrote the constitution and by-laws and became the first president of the organization.

He had married a cousin, Mary Barton of Newton, Massachusetts, and they had twelve children. His interest in medicine continued, and it was this profession that was chosen by three of his sons and seven of his grandsons. Bartlett died in 1795 at the age of sixty-six and was buried in Kingston. The only known statue of him is in his birthplace.

Bartlett was buried in the First Cemetery, Kingston.

Bartlett's house in Kingston, N. H.

WILLIAM WHIPPLE.

General Whipple made his home in Portsmouth.

WILLIAM WHIPPLE was in his forty-seventh year when he cast his vote for the Declaration, being a couple of months younger than his colleague Bartlett. Born in Kittery, later part of the state of Maine though then in Massachusetts, he made his home in Portsmouth, New Hampshire, where he had been a merchant until the dispute with the mother country caused him to enter public life. After prominent local service to the Patriot cause he was sent to the second Continental Congress in 1776. Except for brief intervals of military service, he continued in that body until 1779, being an active and effective committeeman. He commanded contingents of New Hampshire troops at Saratoga and in Rhode Island and has gone down in history as General Whipple. He was a very spirited Patriot and an unfailingly optimistic one. After leaving Congress he was a member of the legislature of his state, and from 1782 until his death in 1785, in his fifty-sixth year, was an associate justice of the superior court, though suffering from ill health. He had married a cousin, Catherine Moffatt of Portsmouth; their only child died in infancy.

It is said that General Whipple, on his way to join the army of General Gates at Saratoga, had with him a slave named Prince, whom he exhorted to fight bravely if they should be called into action. Prince then replied: 'Sir, I have no inducement to fight; but if I had my liberty, I would endeavor to defend it to the last drop of my blood.' The story is that the General freed his slave on the spot.

101

Matthew Thornton.

MATTHEW THORNTON, the third Signer from New Hampshire, was elected to the Continental Congress in September 1776, and arrived in Philadelphia early in November, when he affixed his signature and incurred all the dangers which that act involved. He was older than his two colleagues, being about sixty-two at the time, and, like Bartlett, was a physician. Born in Ireland of Scottish stock, he came with his parents to what is now the state of Maine when about four years old, afterward living near Worcester, Massachusetts. Before he was grown he settled in Londonberry, New Hampshire, in a colony of Ulster Irish. He served as 'under-surgeon' with New Hampshire troops in the Louisburg expedition of 1746, bore the title of Colonel in the militia in later years, became a representative in the provincial legislature in his middle forties, and was active in public life for a generation thereafter. He was prominent in the agitation against the Stamp Act, presided over the provincial congress in 1775, and was chairman of the committee of safety.

He remained in the Continental Congress only about a year. Like Bartlett and Whipple, he became a member of the judiciary of New Hampshire, serving as an associate justice of the superior court until he was sixty-eight. During his seventies he was in the state senate, and after that he retired to his farm in Merrimack County. He and his wife, Hannah Jack,

Thornton's gravestone in Thornton's Ferry Cemetery, Merrimack, N. H.

had five children. He died in Newburyport, Massachusetts, in 1803 while visiting one of them, a daughter. He was eighty-nine at the time. On the marble slab over his grave in Merrimack, New Hampshire, is the inscription, 'An Honest Man.'

He was a large man, with black and penetrating eyes and an 'invincibly grave' expression. His extreme seriousness of mind is shown by the fact that he wrote a metaphysical treatise when over eighty. The title of this unpublished work was: 'Paradise Lost; or the Origin of the Evil, called Sin.'

All five Massachusetts Signers of the Declaration had attended Harvard College.

John Hancock

Sam^d Adams *Robt Treat Paine*
John Adams *Elbridge Gerry*

The Massachusetts delegation of five was comparable in distinction with the larger delegations from Pennsylvania and Virginia and was second to none in influence. Samuel Adams, the oldest member, had probably done more to promote the colonial revolt than had any other man. John Hancock appears to have been the showiest man in Congress, and John Adams was the most effective debater there. Robert Treat Paine, who was next to Samuel Adams in age, is not well known in our day, but he was a man of high contemporary standing. The baby of the group, Elbridge Gerry, was destined to become a controversial figure. All of these men came from eastern Massachusetts, all were graduates of Harvard College, and all were present to vote for the Declaration.

106

JOHN HANCOCK *and Dorothy Quincy were married in 1775.*

JOHN HANCOCK was in his fortieth year when he attached his famous autograph to the Declaration as the President of Congress, and was the richest member of the New England group. The son of a clergyman, he was born at Braintree, not far from the birthplace of John Adams, who knew him from the cradle to the grave. From his uncle, Thomas Hancock, who adopted him, he inherited what was then a vast fortune; and as a young man, according to John Adams, he was 'the delight of the eyes' of the whole town of Boston. The portrait of him by Copley shows how he looked about the time of the Stamp Act, soon after he came into his princely estate. It included a seat on Beacon Hill, which was a good deal higher then than it is now. The main house was a two-story granite structure and the landscaping was the talk of the town. His uncle was a merchant, engaged in far-flung commercial enterprises. His own shipping activities in a more difficult period were considerably less successful, but he retained large holdings of real estate and never ceased to be a man of fortune.

His contemporaries found this 'patriot in purple' extraordinarily generous. According to Samuel Adams, the town of Boston really acquired his fortune when it elected him to public office. In 1769, when he was in his early thirties, he was sent to the General Court, that is, the provincial legislature. That same year he gained great public prominence from the seizure of his sloop *Liberty* by the British, after Madeira wine had been landed from it without payment of duty, while an official was forcibly confined in the cabin. Hancock opposed

Hancock's house is said to have been the first on Beacon Hill.

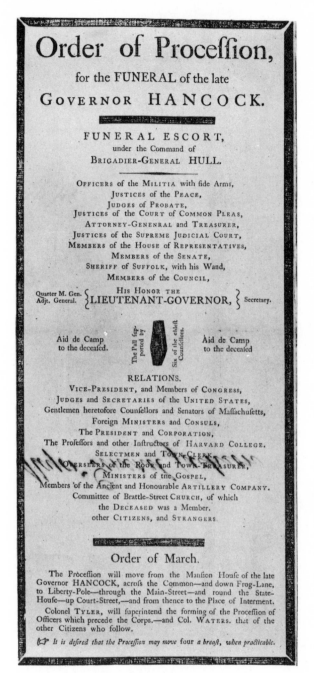

Hancock's funeral was the most impressive New England had seen. The procession ended at Boston's Old Granary Burying Ground.

British regulations in part because they interfered with his extensive commercial transactions, some of which were extra-legal. On the other hand, he risked one of the greatest of colonial fortunes when he took the road to political independence.

John Adams in retrospective old age linked Hancock's name with those of James Otis and Samuel Adams as an 'essential character' in the Revolution, and his fellow Patriots delighted to do him honor. He himself delighted to receive it, for he was a vain man. He was rather spoiled, and at times was peevish, perhaps because of physical infirmity. No doubt his ill health resulted in part from excessively good living, for he suffered particularly from gout. He was nearly six feet tall, with a slender person, and he stooped a little as he grew older. The consensus was that he was an excellent presiding officer.

His most notable later service was as governor of Massachusetts. He was elected to that office nine times and, except for two years, held it without a break from 1780 until his death in 1793 at the age of fifty-six. Some historians have questioned his effectiveness and decisiveness in this office, but he continued to be generous and popular. While he was governor, President George Washington visited Boston, and Hancock's tardiness in making him a ceremonial visit has often been cited as an instance of his own vanity. It may also be explained, however, on the ground that he was genuinely incapacitated from gout.

Toward the end of the summer of 1775, he married Dorothy Quincy. This was a late marriage, but one that befitted his position in all respects. It was without enduring fruit; the only son of this fine couple died at the age of nine and their only daughter died in infancy. Hancock himself had the most impressive funeral ever given a New Englander until that time, and he would have relished the pomp had he been in position to observe it. He has been less honored in memory, but his services to the cause of American independence were great, even though often flamboyant.

Samuel Adams was more interested in the public's business than his own.

SAMUEL ADAMS, the oldest member of the delegation from Massachusetts, was in his fifty-fourth year when the Declaration was adopted, the fulfillment of his fondest hopes. No one had done more and perhaps no one else had done so much in behalf of American rights and liberties. Notoriously indifferent to his private fortunes and ineffectual in his own business, he had made the public business his main concern from his early forties. From the beginnings of the long controversy with the mother country the most fitting designation for him was 'professional patriot.' But the most noted of the pre-Revolutionary agitators was no self-seeker. Unlike John Hancock, he cared nothing for personal glory; to him the cause was paramount, and his most important activities were behind the scenes.

Sam Adams was buried in the Old Granary Burying Ground, ten years after Hancock's burial there.

Born in Boston and educated at Harvard, he was already associated with the popular party, against the 'Court' party, when the Sugar and Stamp Acts gave him his great opportunity. Henceforth the cause of the patriots gave him his effective career. His political arena was the town of Boston and the House of Representatives, in which he served continuously from 1765 until he went to the first Continental Congress in 1774. As clerk of the Massachusetts House he had his eye on everything, and his hand entered into innumerable resolutions. As a leader of the Caucus Club and the Sons of Liberty he kept alive the flame of opposition to the Royal Governors. His verbal attacks on the customs collectors and the British troops helped to create the sentiment that resulted in the Boston Massacre; he initiated town com-

mittees of correspondence; he used Thomas Hutchinson's letters to destroy the influence of that official; and he is credited with the instigation of the Boston Tea Party. He was a major mover for the first Continental Congress and was incessantly active there, gaining support for Massachusetts. It is not at all surprising that the British troops sought to capture him at Lexington. He was one of the earliest and most consistent advocates of independence, and the adoption of the Declaration marked the culmination of his labors and his career.

He was of medium stature, had steel-gray eyes and a prominent nose, and could look stern when the occasion warranted. The artist Copley caught him in a serious moment, but as a rule he was genial, and he was always simple in his tastes. One of his fellow-Signers said: 'His morals were irreproachable, and even ambition and avarice, the usual vices of politicians, seemed to have no place in his breast.' Such was his regard for public worship that during a later period in Congress, when it was meeting at York, Pennsylvania, it is said that he regularly attended services in German, when there were no others, though he was wholly ignorant of the language.

Samuel Adams cannot possibly be omitted from the story of the preliminaries of the Revolution, but, although he lived twenty-seven years longer (until 1803), his later career was unimportant. He continued to serve in Congress until the war was nearing its end; he held local offices in Massachusetts and succeeded John Hancock as governor; he first opposed and then supported the new United States Constitution; but he never could go along with the Federalist party which was becoming dominant in his commonwealth. This supreme agitator lacked constructive statesmanship, and as party lines were drawn in the last decade of the century he really had no place to go. To the end of his days he was a pre-Revolutionary figure. John Adams may have overstated the case when he described Samuel as 'a helpless object of compassion' in his last years, but he sized up his kinsman's public services when he said he was 'born and tempered a wedge of steel to split the knot of *lignum vitae,* which tied North America to Great Britain.' Samuel Adams was 'an original,' and, from his day until ours, historians have delighted to analyze him. He was a one-cause man, and after that cause triumphed he could find no other that commanded him.

He was twice married: first, to Elizabeth Checkley, by whom he had a son and daughter; and, some years after her death, to Elizabeth Wells. He died in Boston in 1803 at the age of eighty-one, and his remains are in the Old Granary Burying Ground. The rough stone over his grave is more in his spirit and character than the more pretentious statue of him in the city where he lived so long.

112

JOHN ADAMS *became second President of the United States.*

The birthplace of John Adams, Quincy, Mass.

JOHN ADAMS, one of the most eminent of early Americans in the full light of history, was a dozen years younger than his kinsman Samuel, being in his forty-first year in the summer of 1776. He was not a tall man, and with the passage of the years he tended more and more to stoutness, but there never was any question of his strength and vigor. He had none of the guile of his kinsman. He was forthright, impulsive, and at times most indiscreet. His defense of the British soldiers after the Boston Massacre was one of the noblest examples of his sense of justice and his personal and political indiscretion. As we have seen, it was during the debates on the Declaration that he was dubbed 'the Atlas of American Independence.'

Born in Braintree (now Quincy), Massachusetts, he was graduated from Harvard, studied and practiced law, and made himself a man of great learning. His marriage to Abigail Smith, when he was twenty-nine, was an event of major importance in his life. This extraordinary woman showed her mettle during the Revolution, when her patriotic husband was long away from home. Beginning in 1778, he was abroad, for the next ten years, with brief intermissions. With Franklin and John Jay, he negotiated the peace treaty with the British, and not until 1784 did Abigail join him in Europe. After a year in France, where Adams served as commercial commissioner with Franklin and Jefferson, he went to England, where he was the first American minister. His friendship with Jefferson, which had its roots in their intimate association in the Continental Congress at the time of the Declaration, now reached full flower. Adams's foreign service was of high distinction, and his election in 1788 as

the first Vice President of the United States—
at a time when that really meant that he
ranked as the second man—was well deserved.

The story of his life from then until 1801 is a
well-known part of the history of his country.
After two terms as Vice President, he became
the second President, being succeeded in that
office by Jefferson, from whom he had become
alienated. The reconciliation of these old
friends, when they were both old men and out
of the political arena, is one of the most pleas-
ing episodes in American history; and the
death of both of them on the same day, the
fiftieth anniversary of the Declaration, was a
strikingly dramatic and symbolic coincidence.
Adams's last recorded words were, 'Thomas
Jefferson still survives,' though, actually, the
younger of the two men died first. Adams lived
to be ninety-one.

He had spent his last years in retirement at
Quincy, on his farm and amid his beloved
books. His own writings on government, though
ponderous and often virtually unreadable, represent a significant contribution to American
political thought. He grew more conservative
as he grew older—from the French Revolution
onward. What he really favored was a bal-
anced government, never going as far as Hamilton in the direction of 'consolidation.' The fire
of liberty which had flamed in the American
Revolution was never smothered in his patriotic breast, and when he and Jefferson engaged in learned correspondence in their last
years both of them were sure that they were
still in the spirit of 1776.

John Adams was the founder of one of the
most eminent of American families. His son
John Quincy became Secretary of State and
President; his grandson Charles Francis was
American minister to Great Britain during the
Civil War; in the third generation appeared
another Charles Francis, Henry, and Brooks,
each in his own way distinguished; and in our
own century another Adams was in the Cab-
inet. John and Abigail lie buried in Quincy and
their old home is a delight to see.

When Abigail Adams died in 1818 her son, John Quincy Adams, wrote in his diary that his father had said, 'the affectionate participation and cheering encouragement of his wife had been his never-failing support.'

R OBERT T REAT P AINE *was called 'The Objection Maker.'*

ROBERT TREAT PAINE, aged forty-five, was next to the oldest member of the Massachusetts delegation. He was born in Boston and could trace his ancestry back to a colonial governor, an acting president of Harvard, and a signer of the Mayflower Compact. He went to Harvard, like the other members of this group. The family tradition pointed to his becoming a clergyman but he turned to the law, making his home in Taunton. His prominence as a patriot and a lawyer was such that he was made one of the prosecutors of the British soldiers after the Boston Massacre, being then opposed by John Adams for the defense. He was a delegate to the first Continental Congress as well as the second, and a very particular friend of John Hancock. He gained some reputation in Congress by his opposition to the proposals of others and was dubbed 'The Objection Maker.' He was, however, an unusually effective committeeman. He had been regarded as a rather more moderate Patriot than the Adamses, for he was not entirely hopeless of conciliation with the mother country, as his signing the 'Olive Branch Petition' had shown. In July 1776, however, he was resolute in support of the Declaration.

Though re-elected to Congress in 1777, he remained in Massachusetts, where he was the first attorney general of the state and shared in the drafting of the first state constitution. In 1780 he removed to Boston and accepted an appointment by Governor Hancock to the state supreme court that he had previously declined. He served until 1804, retiring to spend the remaining ten years of his life 'in daily converse with aristocratic fellow Federalists.' He died in Boston at the age of eighty-three and was buried in Old Granary Burying Ground. He had married Sally Cobb, sister of General David Cobb of the Revolution, and had eight children. The second of these was Robert Treat Paine, the poet, who was long estranged from his strait-laced father because he was associated with the theater and gave other signs of worldliness.

ELBRIDGE GERRY, like John Hancock, was a merchant and at this stage well-to-do. He was thirty-two years old in the summer of 1776 and living at Marblehead, where he was born. He was one of the early advocates of independence and a strong supporter of the Declaration, but because of absence from Congress in August he did not sign until September. His early revolutionary fervor may be attributed in part to the influence of Samuel Adams, whom he met as a representative in the provincial legislature in 1772, a decade after his own graduation from Harvard.

Throughout his life Gerry, though concerned to protect property interests, was anti-British in sentiment and fearful of tyranny. He shared the dangers from the British march on Lexington and Concord; during the night of April 18, 1775, he escaped a detachment of redcoats by fleeing in his nightclothes from an inn at Arlington into a cornfield. As a delegate to the second Continental Congress he went to Philadelphia early in 1776 with John Adams, and he was to maintain a firm friendship with that gentleman through a turbulent generation.

Gerry was a dapper little man with pleasant manners, a rather stern expression, and a tendency to stammer. He was properly esteemed for his integrity, but he lacked humor and had a suspicious nature. His later career was marked by much apparent inconsistency. He served faithfully and effectively in Congress, but absented himself for three years, beginning in

ELBRIDGE GERRY'S *name is perpetuated in the word 'gerrymander.'*

Gerry, who became fifth Vice President of the United States, was born in Marblehead.

1780, though nominally still a member. He eventually returned, and he was a member of the Federal Convention, though he was one of the three delegates present who declined to sign the finished Constitution. In 1789, he went to Congress as a supporter of the Constitution and backed the financial measures of Hamilton. By this time he was making his home in Cambridge.

Retiring from Congress in 1793, he turned against the Federalists, because of his revived anti-British sentiments and fears of tyranny. President John Adams appointed him in 1797 a member of the ill-fated mission to France as a makeweight to the two Federalist members, and he became isolated from his colleagues at the time of the 'X.Y.Z.' affair. The Federalists ostracized him, and his conduct has generally been regarded as unwise, but Adams never questioned his patriotism. Taken up by the Republicans on his return, he was nominated for governor; and, after a succession of defeats, was elected in 1810 and re-elected the next year. It was then that a redistricting bill was passed for the benefit of the Republican party, which

gave rise to the expression 'gerrymander.' One extraordinary election district looked like a salamander, which word was soon modified by the insertion of the Governor's name.

Gerry failed of re-election as governor in 1812, but was nominated for the vice presidency of the United States on the ticket with Madison and elected to that office. He further alienated the dominant group in his own state by staunchly supporting the War of 1812. He died in 1814, in his seventy-first year, being stricken in his carriage on the way to preside over the Senate. He was buried in the Congressional Cemetery at public expense, his fortune having disappeared. He had married Ann Thompson of New York and left three sons and four daughters. A grandson of his attained distinction as a lawyer and philanthropist in New York, and in our own generation his great-grandson was Senator from Rhode Island.

Gerry remains a controversial figure and certainly does not fit into any simple political pattern. John Adams paid him the finest tribute he ever received by remaining his staunch friend through forty years of divisive politics.

It is not surprising that 'Little Rhody' had the smallest number of Signers of the Declaration—only two. Little Delaware had the advantage of propinquity to Philadelphia. Throughout her early history, Rhode Island, always fearful of being dominated by her larger neighbors, was more notable for individualism than for the spirit of co-operation. Yet, having managed to preserve her seventeenth-century charter, she shared with Connecticut the distinction of being more independent of the mother country than any of the royal or proprietary colonies were, and her vigorous participation in the intercolonial movement for full independence was to be expected. It may be noted in passing that she contributed to the common cause the most conspicuous American military figure, next to Washington, in the Revolution—General Nathanael Greene.

STEPHEN HOPKINS, many times colonial governor of Rhode Island, was the senior delegate from the little state and one of the oldest of the Signers, being in his seventieth year when he attached his signature to the Declaration. A descendant of Thomas Hopkins, who was an associate of Roger Williams, he had been born in Cranston and was living in Providence as a merchant. Since the age of twenty-five he had been an office-holder almost continuously; he had served as chief justice among other things, and had been elected governor nine times. A prominent patriot for years, he prevented the arrest of the burners of the *Gaspee,* and was a delegate to the first Continental Congress as well as the second. One of the other delegates to the latter described him as a venerable man 'of an original understanding, extensive reading, and great integrity,' who thoroughly believed in liberty, while fully recognizing its inevitable costliness.

His experience and judgment made him exceedingly useful in congressional business, and John Adams reported that despite his age he kept his colleagues up late talking. Hopkins never drank to excess, said Adams, but all he drank was promptly converted into 'wit, sense, knowledge, and good humor.' He was particularly active on the committee that was drawing up the Articles of Confederation, but he left

Congress in September 1776 because of ill health. He did local public service after that and lived until 1785, when he died in Providence at the age of seventy-eight. A man of literary and scientific interests, despite his lack of formal education, he was the first chancellor of Rhode Island College. He was twice married—to Sarah Scott and Mrs. Anne Smith—and his first wife bore him seven children. Four of his five sons were seagoing. No portrait of him from life has been discovered.

Hopkins lived in Providence, where he engaged in surveying and mercantile pursuits.

123

WILLIAM ELLERY was in his forty-ninth year when he took his seat in Congress in the middle of May 1776. Born in Newport, where he continued to live and was to die, he was a graduate of Harvard and a lawyer. He was noted for his ready wit, and he often amused himself by writing epigrams about his colleagues while they were speaking. According to a well-known story, Ellery, at the signing of the Declaration, took a position where he could watch the faces of the delegates as they put their names to this revolutionary document, and reported afterward that every one of them showed 'undaunted resolution.' His local services to the patriotic cause had occasioned his own election to the second Continental Congress by the Assembly of Rhode Island. From that time onward, elections were by popular vote. Except for two years, he was repeatedly re-elected, serving in Congress until 1786 and being notably diligent as a committeeman.

During the period of the Confederation, Rhode Island, reassuming her historic role, became notorious among the states for independence and individualism. Ellery sympathized with this spirit, but he was appointed to office under the new Federal Constitution before his state had ratified that document. On January 1, 1790, President Washington appointed him collector of customs for the Newport district, and he retained this post, through all the changes in administration, until his death thirty years later. His tastes were notably literary, and he was a prolific letter-writer. He died in 1820 in his ninety-third year and except for Charles Carroll of Carrollton was the longest-lived of the Signers. He married Ann Remington of Cambridge, and, after her death, Abigail Cary. Two of his grandchildren gained renown: the elder Richard Henry Dana, poet and essayist; and William Ellery Channing, the noted Unitarian clergyman.

Roger Sherman   *Wm Williams*

Oliver Wolcott   *Samd Huntington*

The four Signers from Connecticut differed greatly in their origins. Two of them were self-made men; one started as a cobbler, the other as a cooper. Another of them, the son of a colonial governor, was born to local official-dom; while the remaining member, the son of a minister, married into it. The two who lacked formal education acquired a good deal of learning, neverthe-less, and all of them had in common long public service in a colony that had been virtually self-governing for years. As the story runs, Patrick Henry once asked Roger Sherman why the people of Connecticut were more devoted to the cause of liberty than the other colonists; and Sherman replied that they had more to lose than anybody else—their 'beloved charter.' This gave them a degree of freedom from imperial control which only Rhode Island also en-joyed. These four men were all in the prime of life, and there was no ques-tion of their resolute support of full American independence.

125

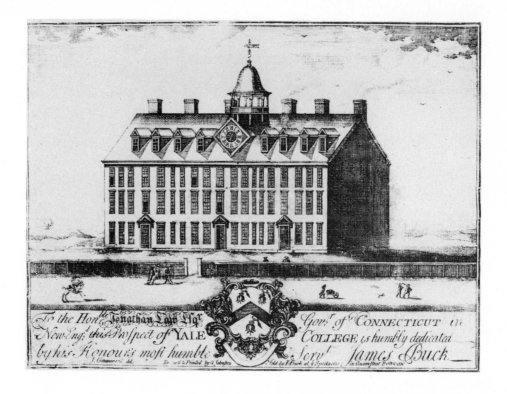

To the Honble Jonathan Law Esqr Govr of CONNECTICUT in New Engd this Prospect of YALE COLLEGE is humbly dedicated by his Honours most humble Servt James Buck

ROGER SHERMAN, the oldest and now the best-known member of the delegation from Connecticut, was also the plainest. Then fifty-five years old, he had been born in Newton, Massachusetts, where he grew up in rather humble circumstances without the benefit of much formal education. He acquired a great love for reading, however, and became in the course of time a well-informed man. He learned the cobbler's trade from his father and began to practice it in New Milford, Connecticut, about the time he was grown. The story is that he walked the whole way with his tools on his back. He soon became a local official, acquired land, became a lawyer and merchant, and at the age of forty he removed to New Haven to engage in large mercantile affairs. Even for his unspecialized age he was notable for the variety of his occupations—and, also, for the number of offices he held concurrently. For about twenty years he was an assistant, or member of the upper house of the legislature,

Among Yale College's graduates was Oliver Wolcott. Another Signer, Roger Sherman, received an honorary degree.

and judge of the superior court. In the course of time he became associated with Yale College and eventually received from that institution the honorary degree of M.A. A strict Puritan and very plain in his dress, as his portrait shows, he was a shrewd and able man.

In the conflict with the mother country, he was generally recognized as a moderate—that is, he did not like violence—but he was one of the earliest to deny the supremacy of Parliament, and he was a member of the first Continental Congress as well as the second. Though he was a member of the committee to draft the Declaration, his hand seems to have left no mark on the document except his signature. He served in Congress throughout most of the Revolution and the period of the Confederation, and was recognized as one of the more influential members. The old Puritan is said to have been 'cunning as the Devil' in legislative processes. His skill was further manifested in the Federal Convention of 1787, where he intro-

126

ROGER SHERMAN.

duced what has come to be known as the Great Compromise of the Constitution. He was the only man known to have signed the Association of 1774, the Declaration of Independence, the Articles of Confederation, and the Constitution. Under the new government he served a term in the House of Representatives and was in the Senate when he died in 1793 at the age of seventy-two.

He was twice married—to Elizabeth Hartwell and Rebecca Prescott—and had fifteen children. He lies buried in Grove Street Cemetery, New Haven, and in that city his name is still well-remembered.

Sherman's home in New Haven.

127

128

OLIVER WOLCOTT.

Oliver Wolcott, son of a colonial governor, married Laura Collins. One of their five children became the second Secretary of the Treasury.

OLIVER WOLCOTT, in his fiftieth year, was the most distinguished of the Connecticut representatives in his person and background. The son of a colonial governor in a virtually self-governing colony, he was born at Windsor, Connecticut, graduated from Yale at the head of his class, and became a lawyer in Litchfield. His home still may be seen in that lovely town. He was a tall, dignified, and urbane man who had often represented Litchfield in the General Assembly and was a member of the upper house without interruption from 1771 to 1786. Because of illness, he left Congress in June 1776, but in July he brought from New York to Litchfield the equestrian statue of George III, and this was largely melted down, for bullets, in the rear of his white house. No doubt this compensated him in his own mind for his inability to vote for the Declaration. He signed the document after his return to Philadelphia in October.

He was elected to Congress almost continuously after that, until the end of the war. He was more active in military than legislative affairs, however, and served first as brigadier general of militia and then as major general. Part of his brigade was with Gates, against Burgoyne. After the war he was commissioner at the Treaty of Fort Stanwix with the Six Nations. He was a strong supporter of the new Constitution of the United States. He served as lieutenant-governor and, for a short time, as governor of Connecticut, dying in the latter office in 1797 at the age of seventy-one. He was a staunch Federalist and a consistent opponent of the doctrines identified by him with the French Revolution.

He had married Laura Collins of Guilford. One of their five children was Oliver Wolcott, Jr., who was associated with Alexander Hamilton in the Treasury Department and succeeded him as Secretary.

William Williams served in the French and Indian War.

WILLIAM WILLIAMS took the place of Oliver Wolcott in Congress when that gentleman left, and Williams probably arrived in time to vote for the Declaration. Forty-five years old, he had resigned a colonel's commission in order to attend. Born in Lebanon, Connecticut, the son of a Congregational minister, he graduated from Harvard and studied theology, but, after serving in the French and Indian War, became engaged in business at Lebanon, where for many years he was a selectman and town clerk. He was a member of the lower house of the legislature for fifteen years before the Declaration; and at the age of forty (1771) he married Mary, daughter of Governor Jonathan Trumbull, thus allying himself with one of the most prominent and influential families in the colony. A man of naturally ardent temper, he threw himself vehemently into the struggle for independence, wielding a vigorous pen and drawing generously on his purse in support of military activities.

Mary Trumbull Williams.

He was a man of the middle stature, erect and well-proportioned, and had black eyes and black hair. Normally he was taciturn, but upon occasion his strong feelings led him into violence of language. After the Declaration he served for a couple of years in Congress; he was a delegate to the state convention of 1788 and voted for the ratification of the Federal Constitution; for nearly a score of years he was a member of the governor's council; and for a generation he was a local judge. He died in Lebanon in 1811 at the age of eighty and was buried there. He had three children.

Williams' home, Lebanon.

132

SAMUEL HUNTINGTON.

The home of Samuel Huntington, Norwich.

SAMUEL HUNTINGTON, whose forty-fifth birthday fell on July 3, 1776, was the youngest member of the Connecticut delegation. Born at Windham, the son of a farmer, he had little schooling and served his apprenticeship as a cooper. He studied law on his own and practiced in Norwich. When the imperial controversy became acute he was a member of the upper house of the legislature and a judge of the superior court, having previously been King's attorney. Beginning in 1775, he represented Connecticut in the Continental Congress for a decade, serving longer than any of the other Signers from his state, and for a couple of years he was president of that body.

Benjamin Rush described him as 'a sensible, candid and worthy man and wholly free from state prejudices.' Also a man of notable simplicity, he was so economical that he was charged by some with parsimony. His record shows un-

Huntington was buried in old Norwichtown Cemetery.

mistakably that he inspired confidence. From 1786 onward he was governor of Connecticut for a dozen years. He strongly supported the United States Constitution and received two electoral votes in the Presidential contest of 1788, when every elector voted for two persons, without distinguishing between the offices of President and Vice President. He married Martha Devotion and, having no children, adopted two children of his brother Joseph. One of these, another Samuel Huntington, became governor of Ohio. The Signer died in 1796 at the age of sixty-five and was buried at Norwich.

Since the delegates from New York in the Continental Congress abstained from the vote on the Declaration of Independence, they played no positive part in the adoption of that charter. Of the four Signers from that state only two—Francis Lewis and William Floyd—were actually present when the vote was taken, and these quiet men would probably have had little to say even if they had been free to speak. The other two, who were more prominent—Philip Livingston and Lewis Morris—were absent at the time. These were all men of wealth, drawing rich sustenance from the land and from commerce. This may be a partial explanation of their relative conservatism, though the sharp division of opinion within their constituency imposed a cautious policy on them. At all events, these men in their own persons certainly provide no warrant for viewing the American Revolution as a class conflict. To them it must have seemed that the struggle was primarily for political independence and self-government; and it is a fact that some of them suffered considerably in their own fortunes for espousing the cause of independence.

135

FRANCIS LEWIS, aged sixty-three, oldest of the Signers from New York, was a retired merchant, living at Whitestone, Long Island. Born in Wales, the son of a clergyman, he was left an orphan while still a child. He had already had mercantile experience when he came to New York at the age of twenty-five; and, after gaining a considerable fortune, he retired from business in his fifties. He was drawn into public life by the exigencies of his times and participated actively in the patriotic movement. In the Continental Congress, however, he was inactive in debate. He and his colleague William Floyd were described as good men who 'never quit their chairs.' Furthermore, the failure of his province to send instructions made it impossible for him to vote for independence on July 2 or the adoption of the full

Declaration on July 4. Though he was a reticent man, his wide experience and good judgment were valuable assets on committees. He did some public service after leaving Congress in 1779, but a couple of years later, when about sixty-eight, he wholly retired.

He had married Elizabeth Annesley of New York, and three of their seven children survived infancy. His house on Long Island was burned by the British and his wife imprisoned. The sufferings she underwent at that time hastened her death, and the war is said to have impaired his fortunes. He was nearly ninety when he died in New York in 1802. His longevity has been ascribed to his habitual temperance.

The only Signer buried in Manhattan, Lewis rests in an unidentified grave in Trinity churchyard, Wall Street and Broadway. The church shown was built in 1846.

438

PHILIP LIVINGSTON.

PHILIP LIVINGSTON, in his sixty-first year, would have been an impressive figure in any gathering. A member of one of the greatest of the manorial families of the province of New York, he enjoyed throughout life the privileges of great wealth and was notable in his locality for his acceptance of the attendant responsibilities. Born at Albany and educated at Yale —when there was no college in his own province—he established himself as an importer in New York City and greatly profited from his mercantile ventures. Besides his town house he had a country place on Brooklyn Heights and from there he was able to see with ease his own

From his house on Brooklyn Heights Livingston could see his ships in the harbor.

ships plying the harbor. This stern eighteenth-century aristocrat, whose ample figure implied good living, interested himself generously in public causes. He was one of the earliest advocates of the establishment of King's College (later Columbia), although as a Presbyterian he did not like its Anglican connections. He aided in the organization of the New York Society Library, served on the first board of the New York Hospital, and was noted for his own philanthropies. He also performed public service as an alderman and as a representative in the provincial Assembly, where for a time he was Speaker.

As a member of the powerful Livingston family he was drawn into their conflict with the De Lanceys and associated with the more popular party. From the time of the Stamp Act a strong opponent of the British policy, he denied the right of Parliament to tax the colonists without their consent and advocated self-government. He had no sympathy, however, with the riotous actions of the Sons of Liberty and must be identified with the conservative wing of the Patriot party. He strongly opposed the Coercive Acts of 1774, went as a delegate to the first Continental Congress, and was a member of the committee to enforce the Association. It is uncertain just what position he would have taken had he been present at the debates on the Declaration in

MRS. LIVINGSTON.

June and July, 1776, but he signed the document in August and cast his lot with the revolution. He was attending a later session of Congress, at York, Pennsylvania, when he died in 1778 at the age of sixty-two, and he was buried there.

It is hard to keep in mind the relationships between the various members of the Livingston clan, which gave to the country so many distinguished men. Philip was the grandson of Robert, first lord of the manor; the brother of William Livingston, the first governor of the state of New Jersey; and the cousin of Robert R. Livingston, chancellor of New York and minister to France at the time of the Lou-

isiana Purchase. Both William and Robert R. Livingston were also members of the second Continental Congress. The former left early in June to assume command of the New Jersey militia. The latter was a member of the committeee of five to draft the Declaration, but he had regarded its adoption as inexpedient at the time and had left Congress when the acceptance of it by New York was reported to Congress. He did valuable service for the revolutionary cause afterward but never signed the document.

Philip Livingston married Christina Ten Broeck of Albany, and this aristocratic couple had five sons and three daughters.

LEWIS MORRIS, fifty years old, lord of the manor of Morrisania in Westchester County, was and remained until his death a representative of the landed aristocracy that flowered along the Hudson. Born at Morrisania and, like Philip Livingston, educated at Yale, this heir to a princely estate manifested to an unusual degree the aristocratic graces. Tall and handsome in person, he was courteous in manner and generous in spirit. He greatly enhanced his already great fortune by marrying Mary Walton, and they had ten children—the support of whom involved no problem.

The surprising thing is that this favored

child of fortune, who had lived so pleasantly as a country gentleman, should have identified himself with the hazardous movement for independence. To some extent he was involved in the factional struggle between the Livingstons and the De Lanceys, on the side of the former, and he found himself opposed by many of his Westchester neighbors, who tended to be Loyalists and were on the other side. He had condemned British policy as a member of the Assembly and was active in the movement for a provincial convention in the spring of 1775. He was elected by that body as a delegate to the second Continental Congress. He served effectively on committees, dealing particularly with military matters and Indian affairs. In June 1776, he took leave from Congress to assume command of the Westchester militia, with the rank of brigadier general, but, as things turned out, there was little for him to do.

Though absent from the Continental Congress when the Declaration was adopted, he was a member of the provincial congress of New York which approved it, and he signed it after he got back to Philadelphia in September. He remained in Congress for some months, but during the remaining years of the Revolution and

Morris's marriage to Mary Walton increased his already considerable fortune.

the rest of his life his public service was local. He devoted himself chiefly to his restored estate after the war was over. As a member of the state convention, he strongly supported Alexander Hamilton in the terrific fight over the ratification of the United States Constitution. He died at Morrisania in 1798 when nearly seventy-two years of age. He was a half-brother of Gouverneur Morris, the son of his father's second marriage, who had his own share of the family charm but who, in the full light of history, seems a less attractive figure.

142

Home of Lewis Morris, Morrisania.

WILLIAM FLOYD, in his forty-second year, was the youngest of the Signers from New York and an inconspicuous member of Congress. The Floyds, who were of Welsh descent on the paternal side, had long been established on Long Island. There, at Brookhaven, William was born. He received relatively little school-ing but inherited a large estate and rose to the rank of major general in the militia of his county. He served in the first, as well as the second, Continental Congress, playing no part in the debates, but, according to a member of another delegation, always voting with 'the zealous friends of liberty and independence.'

In his later years Floyd made his home in Westernville, Oneida County, New York.

There was nothing particularly striking about his appearance, and his dignity and reserve discouraged familiarity. When the British occupied Long Island in 1776 his family was forced to flee to Connecticut, where they remained through the Revolution. He was twice married—to Hannah Jones and Joanna Strong—and had five children altogether. His daughter Catherine ("Kitty") was once engaged to James Madison.

He served in Congress throughout most of the Revolution, was a state senator, and had one term in the United States Congress under the Constitution. After that he continued to participate in public affairs but held no other important office. He was practically ruined by the Revolution, and at the age of sixty-nine, revealing notable resiliency, he re-moved to upstate New York. He died at Westernville in 1821 in his eighty-seventh year. The home of his old age is pictured here.

144

John Hart

Jno Witherspoon   *Abra Clark*

Richd Stockton   *Fras Hopkinson*

The Signers from New Jersey comprise one of the more interesting state groups. In June 1776 the provincial congress of New Jersey ousted and arrested the royal governor, William Franklin, then wholly estranged from his father, Benjamin Franklin, who described him as a 'thorough government man.' At the same time the provincial congress elected a fresh delegation of five to the Continental Congress, empowering them to vote for independence. Thus the latter body was reinforced by 'five independent souls,' as John Adams called them. Though one in spirit and purpose, they were unusually diverse as persons. Along with the well-known John Witherspoon of Princeton and Richard Stockton, who had induced him to come to America from Scotland, the delegation contained two very plain men, John Hart and Abraham Clark, along with Francis Hopkinson, whose diversity of gifts extended to literary satire and music.

145

146

JOHN HART.

JOHN HART, at sixty-five the oldest Signer from New Jersey, was a farmer, living at Hopewell, who also owned grist and fulling mills. Born in Stonington, Connecticut, he had come to New Jersey with his parents as a child, and had received little schooling. Becoming a man of importance in his locality, nonetheless, he served continuously in the provincial Assembly for a decade and was a member of successive provincial congresses. Elected with four others to the Continental Congress in June 1776, he voted for the Declaration in early July and signed the engrossed parchment in early August. About this time he was elected to the first Assembly under the new state constitution and was unanimously chosen Speaker. His lands were laid waste and his mill property was badly damaged early in the war and he himself was for a time a fugitive from the British invaders. His health became impaired and he died in 1779 at the age of sixty-eight, before independence had been won.

John Hart married Deborah Scudder and had a large family. He is said to have been a man of medium height and well proportioned, with very black hair and light eyes, and to have been called handsome in his youth. His fellow-Signer, Benjamin Rush, described him as 'a plain, honest, well meaning Jersey farmer, with but little education, but with good sense and virtue enough to pursue the true interests of his country.'

Hart was buried in the First Baptist Churchyard at Hopewell.

147

148

JOHN WITHERSPOON *was the only clergyman in the Congress.*

A North-West Prospect of Nassau-Hall, with a Front View of the Presidents House, in New-Jersey.

This northwest prospect of Nassau Hall and the President's House appeared shortly before Witherspoon became president of Princeton College.

JOHN WITHERSPOON, President of the College of New Jersey at Princeton and the only clergyman in Congress, then in his fifty-fourth year, would have been a striking figure anywhere. It has been said that he was one of the few men of his time who could be compared to George Washington in 'presence.' Middle-sized and inclined to be stout, he was regarded by many as homely, but he bore himself with grave dignity. This Scottish divine, born near Edinburgh, who had been induced by Richard Stockton and Benjamin Rush to come to America seven or eight years before the Declaration of Independence, generally disapproved the participation of ministers in politics. Until 1774 he had devoted himself to the College, which flourished under him, and to the Presbyterian Church in America, which he did much to stimulate and unify during this and later periods. He is generally credited with introduc-

John Witherspoon lived here in Princeton.

ing the philosophy of 'common sense' into the New World, and many of his pupils, including James Madison, afterward distinguished themselves in public life. The robust practicality of this learned man, who laid such emphasis on the mastery of English and on the public values of education, was well adapted to the American scene. Also, in a critical time, it led to his effective participation in public affairs.

He contributed to the cause of the Patriots by sermons and writings and by participation in various local activities, including membership in provincial congresses. He was a leader in the movement that led to the removal of Governor William Franklin, and was one of the

five 'independent souls' sent to the Continental Congress by New Jersey late in June 1776. In a speech on July 2, when the crucial resolution of independence was being debated, he asserted that the country was 'not only ripe for the measure but in danger of rotting for the want of it.' He was a luminous speaker, in spite of his Scottish accent, and he was indefatigable as a committeeman during his service in Congress. He remained there until 1782, at a time when the conditions of war made it impossible to do much for the College. Perhaps his 'ecclesiastical character' was something of a handicap to him in public life, but his activities on the board of war and the committee on secret correspondence (foreign affairs) were of the first importance. This 'common-sense' philosopher and zealous but never illiberal Patriot proved himself an able statesman.

For a dozen years after the war he devoted himself to the restoration of the College. For a time he was in the state legislature and he was a member of the New Jersey convention that ratified the Federal Constitution. Also, he was chiefly responsible for the national organization of the Presbyterian Church, and presided as moderator at the opening session of the first General Assembly in 1789. In a magazine article in 1781, this Scottish preacher, who had ob-

served the use and abuse of the English tongue in two worlds, coined the term 'Americanism.'

He died in 1794, in his seventy-second year, and lies buried in the President's Lot at Princeton, where his name is properly revered. His first wife, Elizabeth Montgomery, who had been so reluctant to come to the wilds of America, bore him ten children. Of these, five survived infancy and one was killed while serving as an officer in the Continental Army. After her death, Witherspoon, in his old age, married Ann, the young widow of Dr. Armstrong Dill, and by her he had two daughters, one of whom died in infancy.

Witherspoon's grave, President's Lot, Princeton.

RICHARD STOCKTON, who in 1776 was a handsome man of forty-five, was born in Princeton. The College of New Jersey was removed to that place largely through the influence of his father, but he himself graduated from it while it was still at Newark. He studied law and became conspicuously successful in practice, avoiding politics while establishing himself at the bar. He rendered important service to the College, afterward known as Princeton, before becoming active on the public stage. In 1767, as a trustee, he went on a mission to Scotland that resulted in the acceptance of the presidency of the College by the Reverend John Witherspoon, after the opposition of the latter's wife had been finally overcome with the aid of Benjamin Rush, then a medical student in Edinburgh. This was an exceedingly important event in the history of higher education in America. Stockton was a pillar of strength to the College throughout his life, and he was eager to bring its graduates into public affairs.

He himself was drawn into them increasingly

as the struggle with the mother country progressed. He served as a member of the Council of New Jersey, became a justice of the supreme court, and in June 1776 was elected to the Continental Congress as an 'independent soul.' He declined to become chief justice of his state in order to remain in Congress, but his public career was unhappily foreshortened by military developments in his locality. Returning from an inspection of the northern army in the autumn of 1776 to find his state overrun by the British, he removed his family to safety but was himself betrayed to the enemy and held for some months in brutal captivity while his home was pillaged. Congress formally remonstrated against his treatment and he was exchanged, but his health was wrecked and he remained an invalid until his death at his family place, Morven, in 1781. He was then in only his fifty-first year.

He had married Annis Boudinot, a poet in her own right and sister of Elias Boudinot, who married Stockton's sister. Of his six children, his

Annis Boudinot Stockton.

son Richard became an eminent lawyer and prominent Federalist leader, and his daughter Julia married Dr. Benjamin Rush, also a Signer of the Declaration. In person, Stockton was tall and commanding, and he was dignified in manner. He was an accomplished horseman, a graceful speaker, and a cultivated man. He was not a Patriot of the riotous type, being a notable champion of law and order, but he was devoted to the interests of his country and suffered greatly in his own person for the cause of independence.

The home of Richard Stockton.

153

ABRAHAM CLARK, who was fifty when he signed the Declaration, was unquestionably a 'man of the people.' He was born at Elizabethtown, New Jersey, where he continued to live, and he received only a smattering of education. He became a surveyor and came to be known as 'The Poor Man's Counselor,' whether he was ever admitted to the bar or not. His sharp comments on the pretensions of lawyers won him enemies but also gained for him much popular approval. His colleague in Congress, Dr. Benjamin Rush, described him as 'a sensible but cynical man' who was uncommonly quick to see the 'weakness and defects of public men and measures.' Very likely he exploited these to his own political advantage, but undoubtedly he was a champion of popular rights.

After serving as sheriff of Essex County and clerk of the colonial Assembly, Clark, espousing the Patriot cause, became a member and secretary of the provincial committee of safety, and a delegate to the convention that drafted the first constitution of the state. His election in June 1776 as one of the five delegates to the Continental Congress showed that he was a recognized advocate of independence, and he voted for the Declaration without any hesitancy. He remained in Congress for several years, being notably attentive to business and good at drawing reports and resolutions.

His legislative service, in his state and out of it, was practically continuous. He vigorously upheld the rights of New Jersey against the commercial practices of New York in the Confederation period, but he also urged the strengthening of the Union. He was one of the few attendants at the Annapolis Convention of 1786, and only ill health prevented his attendance at the Federal Convention in 1787. He opposed the Constitution until assured of the addition of the Bill of Rights to it, and he was a member of the second and third Congresses un-

Clark's home, at Elizabeth, was unpretentious.

der the new government. Toward the end of his service he strongly supported the policy of commercial discrimination against the British advocated by Madison and Jefferson and defeated by partisans of Hamilton. He was thus identified with the Republicans rather than the Federalists, and his career as a whole fits into the economic interpretation of the politics of the era better than those of most other Signers.

He died in 1794 in his sixty-ninth year and was buried in the Presbyterian Church Cemetery at Rahway. He had married Sarah Hatfield, who bore him ten children and after his death continued to direct the family farm he had inherited. He was a slender man of average height and the miniature by James Peale confirms contemporary comments about the heaviness of his eyebrows.

155

Clark died in Rahway and was buried there.

FRANCIS HOPKINSON, who at thirty-eight was one of the younger Signers, was also one of the most versatile and engaging men in Congress. He is more often associated with Philadelphia, where he was born and died, than with New Jersey, where he was living in 1776 at Bordentown on the Delaware. His father was a prominent Philadelphia lawyer and one of the founders of the American Philosophical Society. Francis was the first graduate of the College of Philadelphia (later affiliated with the University of Pennsylvania) and he studied and practiced law, without repressing his musical, literary, and artistic talents. He played the harpsichord and was himself a composer. For example, in his early thirties he set to music a poem of Thomas Parnell, renaming the song 'My Days Have Been So Wondrous Free.' He also wrote verse and was good at drawing—in which he had apparently received instruction from Benjamin West while on a trip to England.

The decade before the Revolution found him in New Jersey, where he held minor public posts and at the age of thirty-one married Ann Borden. He subsequently removed to Bordentown, which was named for his wife's prominent family. There he practiced law successfully and achieved sufficient political prominence to be appointed a member of the Governor's Council in 1774. A staunch Whig, he soon began to write satirical pieces against the British; and in an essay called 'A Prophecy' he anticipated the Declaration before voting for it. During his brief stay in Congress he whiled away the tedium of debate by drawing caricatures. Below average in height, he had a small head and small, keen features. He was a fast talker and exceedingly animated, some part of him being always in motion.

During the Revolution he attended to much vexatious public business as chairman of the Continental navy board and as treasurer of loans; and, beginning in 1779, he was judge of admiralty for Pennsylvania. This talented man helped design the seals of the American Philosophical Society and the state of New Jersey, and, what is even more interesting, he designed the American flag (1777). His house in Bordentown was plundered by the British soldiers when they occupied Philadelphia. He continued to satirize the enemy and support the American cause in his writings in prose and verse, and he wrote and composed a cantata in celebration of the French Alliance. He strongly supported the new Federal Constitution and directed the great procession in Philadelphia in honor of its ratification by Pennsylvania. In 1789 President Washington appointed him judge of the United States Court for the eastern district of that state, and he held this post until his sudden death two years later in his fifty-fourth year.

An intimate friend of Franklin and the astronomer David Rittenhouse, he was a member

457

FRANCIS HOPKINSON.

*Among Hopkinson's compositions was the music for a poem by Thomas
Parnell. Hopkinson's son, Joseph, was the author of 'Hail Columbia.'*

of the select scientific circle that centered in the American Philosophical Society and was himself a minor inventor. He corresponded extensively with his friend Thomas Jefferson—discussing his own efforts to improve the quilling of the harpsichord, among other things—and this lively man of such diverse gifts must have been one of the most delightful of companions. He was secretary of the convention that organized the Protestant Episcopal Church in 1789, and was the organist of Christ Church. The eldest of his five children, Joseph Hopkinson, a noted jurist, was the author of 'Hail Columbia' (1798). Francis Hopkinson Smith, grandson of the Signer, also carried on the tradition of versatility; besides being an engineer, he was a novelist and painter.

Mrs. Francis Hopkinson.

During the British occupation of Philadelphia redcoats plundered Hopkinson's home in Bordentown.

Benj. Franklin

Geo. Taylor

John Morton

Jas. Smith

James Wilson

Geo. Ross

Rob't Morris

Geo Clymer

Benjamin Rush

159

No other state approached Pennsylvania in the number of Signers, but the length of her list was owing to geography and historical circumstances rather than revolutionary ardor. Actually, she was one of the sisters whose attitude was most uncertain, until the last moment. As late as July 1, 1776, a majority of her delegates were opposed to the resolution of independence. According to John Adams, this was because of 'the timidity of two overgrown fortunes.' He was referring to Robert Morris and John Dickinson, and on July 2 these two men voluntarily absented themselves. Two of the five remaining delegates were against the resolution, but Franklin, John Morton, and James Wilson comprised a majority and they swung Pennsylvania into line. The other two never signed the Declaration, nor did John Dickinson, but Robert Morris did. Late in July, the provincial congress added five new representatives—Taylor, Smith, Ross, Clymer, and Rush—and these men signed in due course.

Thus there were nine Signers from Pennsylvania, and they comprise a richly diverse group. Secretary Charles Thomson, from that state, attested the signature of John Hancock in the first place, but his name did not appear on the engrossed parchment. The final order of signatures within the Pennsylvania group was without significance, and for better understanding we follow a different order here—beginning with the three men who actually voted for the Declaration and taking the others up in the order of age. The result is that we start with Benjamin Franklin and end with Benjamin Rush, two of the most interesting men in Congress. Between these fall three Georges, two named James, and one Robert—the richest of them all. An amazing group by any reckoning.

461

BENJAMIN FRANKLIN.

BENJAMIN FRANKLIN, who was half a year past seventy, was the oldest Signer and the most eminent. Born in Boston, the tenth son of Josiah Franklin and the youngest son of the youngest son for five generations, he picked up most of his early education in a printing shop and made his famous entry into Philadelphia at the age of seventeen. The events of his life from that time forward comprise one of the best, and best-known, of all American success stories. By the age of forty-two he had followed his own maxims sufficiently to acquire a competence that enabled him to give up the management of his printing business and pursue thereafter his manifold personal and public interests. As Poor Richard, he had made his name a household word, and he had already given innumerable manifestations of his passion for self-improvement and the advancement of society.

He was chiefly responsible for the establishment of the first circulating library in America, for the founding of the American Philosophical Society for the Promotion of Useful Knowledge, and, a little later, for the setting up of an academy out of which the University of Pennsylvania developed. Long a clerk of the provincial Assembly, he was thereafter an elected member from Philadelphia. He had his hand in pretty nearly everything in his city and province; and eventually, as deputy postmaster gen-

eral for the colonies, he visited practically every one of them. He was the author of the Albany Plan of Union (1754) and had great capacity for co-operation.

His *Experiments and Observation on Electricity, made in Philadelphia,* which provided an enduring foundation for his fame as a scientist, was published when he was forty-five, and he already enjoyed an international reputation when he went to England in his fifties as an agent of the Pennsylvania Assembly, to represent it before the British government against the Proprietor. During the five years that he was abroad on this mission his scientific fame came into full flower; and, having received honorary degrees from Saint Andrews and Oxford, this self-educated man was commonly referred to thenceforth as 'Doctor.' It was shortly before his return home in 1762, when he was fifty-six, that the philosopher David Hume wrote him: 'I am very sorry that you intend soon to leave our hemisphere. America has sent us many good things, gold, silver, sugar, tobacco, indigo, &c.; but you are the first philosopher, and indeed the first great man of letters for whom we are beholden to her.'

After a year or two in America he returned to England for another decade, during which he represented various colonies at the seat of the home government. Remaining there until 1775, he had the advantage over most of his

Franklin in his 'Autobiography' said that the first time he saw his future wife he was walking up the street eating. He had 'a great puffy roll' under each arm and was munching a third. The strange girl standing in a doorway 'thought I made as I certainly did a most awkward ridiculous appearance.'

Elected to the second Continental Congress the day after he got back to Philadelphia, he served on the committee that drafted the Declaration, and he left his mark on that document even though he did not get the chance to insert a joke in it. He was no man to make speeches, but he was generally regarded as an oracle of wisdom, though John Adams, and others, never could understand why he favored a unicameral legislature; the Pennsylvania constitution of 1776, which he thoroughly approved, was too democratic and too feeble for the liking of many of his fellow Patriots.

The most distinguished of his many political services still lay before him. Sent to France in 1776, when he described himself as a piece of unsalable cloth which could be had for the asking, he was the major architect of the French Alliance and became in French eyes the most famous and beloved of world figures. His later services in connection with the peace treaty and as the first American minister to France need not concern us here, but we can say that he was the dean of American diplomats in his own time and one of the very greatest of all time. Some of his contemporaries were jealous of him, not unnaturally, and his ways seemed devious to some, but to his successor at Versailles he and Washington were in a class by themselves. Jefferson, who was secretary of state when Franklin died in 1790 at the age of eighty-four, suggested that the executive department wear mourning for him, but President Washington wondered where the line could be drawn if ever that sort of thing was started. 'I told him,' said Jefferson, 'the world had drawn so broad a line between himself and Dr. Franklin, on the one side, and the residue of mankind, on the other, that we might wear mourning for them, and the question still remain new and undecided as to all others.'

No other American of the first rank, except Jefferson himself, embodied so fully the dauntless intellectual freedom, the eager intellectual curiosity, and the persistent faith in human progress which characterized the eighteenth-century Enlightenment; and perhaps no other

American compatriots in that he could view the developing imperial controversy firsthand in the home country itself. He was conciliatory as long as he could be, but his admiration for the English declined as time went on, and he was publicly assailed for his connection with the publication of the Hutchinson Letters. In the end nobody was more convinced than he of the desirability of colonial independence. He had never had much use for the proprietors of Pennsylvania and he had lost any he may have had for kings. Jefferson first heard from him the motto, 'Rebellion to tyrants is obedience to God,' and the chances are that Franklin was the author of it.

About ten months before his death in 1790, Franklin asked that a marble stone, 'six feet long, four feet wide, plain,' be placed on his grave. It is to be found in the northwest corner of Christ Church Churchyard, Philadelphia.

great American of any period has ever been so consistently amiable and irrepressibly delightful as Franklin. In his personal life he did not hesitate to be irregular. By Deborah Reed, his common-law wife who was a faithful helpmate though quite incapable of understanding him, he had two children. One of these became the mother of Benjamin Franklin Bache, later rather notorious as a journalist. Franklin had two illegitimate children, one of whom was William Franklin, royal governor of New Jersey. In religious matters he was notably tolerant. In the last year of his life, replying to the letter of a learned clergyman, he said that he was not now disposed to enter into theological inquiry since he would soon have the opportunity to learn the truth without much trouble. Within a month he went to meet his Creator. If not the most heroic and statuesque of Americans, he was, except for Jefferson, the most versatile among the greatest of them and, without any exception, the most entertaining.

JOHN MORTON, who was about fifty-two years old in 1776, was a plain farmer with long political experience and recent judicial service. Born of Swedish stock in Ridley, Pennsylvania, in Chester (now in Delaware) County, he was rather well educated at home by his stepfather. He served almost continuously in the provincial Assembly from his early thirties, and in 1774 became an associate judge of the supreme court. He was a delegate to the first as well as to the second Continental Congress, and in the latter he joined with Franklin and James Wilson to swing the Pennsylvania delegation to the side of independence. The story is that some of his closest friends greatly blamed him for this act and that on his deathbed he said: 'Tell them that they will live to see the hour, when they shall acknowledge it to have been the most glorious service that I ever rendered my country.'

He died in April 1777, less than a year after the Declaration, the first among the Signers to die. At the time he was serving usefully in Congress, but it was still too early to say that the wisdom of his conduct had been conclusively proved. His wife, Ann Justice (or Justis) was also of Delaware Swedish stock. They had three sons and five daughters. Morton died in Chester and was buried in St. James Church Cemetery there.

The birthplace of John Morton.

JAMES WILSON, who was approaching thirty-four, was next to the youngest of the Signers from Pennsylvania and one of the ablest men in Congress. Born at Carskero, near St. Andrews, Scotland, he studied at the universities of St. Andrews, Glasgow, and Edinburgh, and, although he does not appear to have taken a degree, he was an unusually well-educated man when he emigrated to America in his early twenties. Coming to Philadelphia, he studied law under John Dickinson. He eventually moved to Carlisle, where he developed a large legal practice among the Scots-Irish in that district and began the land speculations that were to extend through his life and prove his undoing. Notably a student and thinker, he was

among the first to deny all authority of Parliament over the colonies and to see in the King the only tie of empire, thus anticipating, as Jefferson did, the later British Commonwealth. A pamphlet of his on that subject was widely circulated and very influential. In the second Continental Congress he became more conservative, being one of those who advocated (in June 1776) postponement of the issue of independence. Nevertheless, on July 2 he was one of the three Pennsylvanians who favored decisive action, and he joined with Franklin and John Morton to cast the vote of his province for the fateful resolution.

Wilson was about six feet tall, very erect, and dignified in manner. His sternness of expression

The home of James Wilson.

has been attributed to his extreme shortsightedness. It is doubtful if 'James of Caledonia' was ever a popular figure, but he was a powerful logician and an uncommonly impressive speaker. His younger colleague, Benjamin Rush, said: 'His mind, while he spoke, was one blaze of light. Not a word ever fell from his lips out of time, or out of place, nor could a word be taken from or added to his speeches without injuring them.' He was an effective member of Congress until the autumn of 1777, but he was then removed because of his lack of sympathy with the existing state government.

Becoming increasingly conservative, he violently attacked the democratic Pennsylvania constitution of 1776 and made himself exceedingly unpopular with the majority. For a time he absented himself in Maryland, and with his removal to Philadelphia in 1778 he became closely identified with the aristocratic and moneyed faction, arousing such hostility that he was the victim of mob violence. He again became active in public life with the conservative reaction following the Revolution, and he rendered his most conspicuous public services in the movement for a new federal constitution. In the Federal Convention of 1787 he was second in influence only to James Madison; he played a commanding part in the ratification fight in Pennsylvania, which was marked by some highhanded action; and he was the author of the more conservative state constitution of 1790.

In view of his services and great legal learning, he was naturally commended for high judicial appointment under the new government, and he duly became one of the first associate justices of the Supreme Court. In several respects he anticipated John Marshall in his nationalism. His most notable opinion was in Chisholm *vs.* Georgia, against the state; and it led, by way of reaction, to the eleventh amendment to the Constitution, wherein the right of citizens of one state to sue another state in the federal courts is denied. Wilson, who, as he himself said, was hunted 'like a wild beast' by his creditors, died at Edenton, North Carolina, in 1798, a few weeks before his fifty-sixth birthday. He had greatly over-extended himself as a land speculator and was in a very distressed mental state. In our own century his remains were reinterred in Christ Churchyard, Philadelphia; and we can now estimate more dispassionately than his contemporaries could the public services of this notable early thinker, who wrecked his own career by excessive ambition.

About the time he settled at Carlisle, he married Rachel Bird. One of their six children, Bird Wilson, a judge in Pennsylvania, who left the bench because of his repugnance to capital punishment and became an Episcopal clergyman and theologian, edited his father's works. As a widower in his early fifties, James Wilson married Hannah Gray, but their only child died in infancy and soon thereafter financial storms burst upon him.

167

ROBERT MORRIS, in his forty-third year, was the richest of the Pennsylvania Signers. His partner, Thomas Willing, also a member of the delegation, voted against the resolution of independence and never signed the Declaration. The objections of Morris, who absented himself, were to the timing of the act rather than to the act itself; and, re-elected in July (as Willing was not), he duly signed in August. Actually, his autograph stands first among those of the Pennsylvanians. The possession of a great fortune did not prevent his taking the side of the Patriots, but throughout his public life he was charged by his critics and enemies with furthering his private interests. John Adams, who never had a fortune, did not doubt that Morris pursued mercantile ends, but regarded him as an honest man and an exceedingly useful member of Congress. George Washington relied greatly on the 'financier of the Revolution,' and in 1789 gave him the opportunity, which he declined, to become the first secretary of the treasury.

Mrs. Morris.

Born in Liverpool, Morris came at the age of thirteen to America, where his father of the same name was then engaged in the exportation of tobacco on Chesapeake Bay. The boy was sent to Philadelphia, where he had slight schooling, but, entering a mercantile house, became at a surprisingly early age a partner in the firm of Willing, Morris & Company. This was the first big step upward on the ladder that led this largely self-made man to dizzy financial heights. The activities of an important merchant in those days extended to shipping and banking, and the enterprises of Morris were always far-flung. At a later time he had a monopolistic contract with the Farmers General for the importation of tobacco into France, and in the last years of his life he was disastrously involved in speculation in western lands.

Large in person, agreeable and lavishly hospitable in private life, he was more respected and feared as a public man than he was liked. One of his colleagues said that because of his proud and passionate nature he had 'virulent enemies, as well as affectionate friends.' He was frequently afflicted with asthma, and it is said that as a cure he often resorted to exercises at the pump, laboring as though he were trying to save a sinking vessel. This is also a good description of his activities as a public financier, for the Continental treasury was often at the point of foundering. Though not an orator he was a bold speaker; in a public assembly, as elsewhere, he was the sort of man who overwhelmed the opposition.

His service to the colonial cause began during the controversy over the Stamp Act, and

169

was significantly resumed in 1775 during the final crisis. In Congress he was particularly concerned with the procurement of munitions, and in the work of the committee on secret correspondence, which dealt with American agents abroad; and, toward the end of his early service, he was chairman of the committee on finance. Retiring from Congress in the autumn of 1778, he was charged with fraud by Thomas Paine and others, and his public standing suffered despite his exoneration. His most important later service was as superintendent of finance (1781-84). The term 'dictator' was applied to him in this position, and he was often referred to as the 'Financier.' He had stipulated that he must be left free to carry on his private operations, but these aroused criticism; and inevitably he made enemies in his conduct of the public business in a period when the finances of the government were in a parlous state. He ended his work in a spirit of despair, but he had kept the ship from sinking.

He was a member of the Annapolis Convention of 1786 and of the Federal Convention which followed it. He played an unimportant part in the framing of the Constitution, but he strongly supported it. He was unwilling to assume responsibility for the finances of the new government, but as one of the first senators from his state, serving until 1795, he strongly backed the policies of Alexander Hamilton. His own fortunes collapsed soon thereafter, chiefly because of his immense purchases of unsettled lands, and in 1798 he was arrested for debt. He had sought refuge from his creditors in his country place, 'The Hills' on the Schuylkill, but he spent the next three and a half years in prison. The last five, until his death in 1806 at the age of seventy-two, were passed in obscure retirement. His fall was as spectacular as his rise, and a good deal quicker.

Morris married Mary White, sister of William White, the first Protestant Episcopal bishop of Pennsylvania, and the couple had five sons and two daughters. He is buried in Christ Churchyard, Philadelphia.

Morris vainly sought refuge from his creditors at his country home, 'The Hills.'

He served less than a year in Congress and was relatively inactive. In March 1777, he was elected to the new Supreme Executive Council of the state, but he occupied his post only a few weeks before retiring on account of illness. He died early in 1781, when he was about sixty-five, and was buried in Easton. He had married Mrs. Anne Taylor Savage, who died in 1768. Their only child who survived infancy predeceased his father.

Taylor's house, Easton.

GEORGE TAYLOR, aged sixty, was the oldest of the five new delegates from Pennsylvania who were elected in late July and signed the Declaration in August. He seems to have been born in northern Ireland, and he made his home in Easton, in Northampton County, though his business interests were chiefly at Durham in Bucks County, where he had an iron furnace. His political activities have not been well remembered, and presumably they were not of major importance. A member of the provincial faction that favored the proprietary government, he was a constant opponent of the British in imperial matters from 1763 onward, and in this sense he may be described as a 'furious Whig.' He served a half dozen years in the provincial Assembly, and then, after several years of inactivity, was aroused by the Coercive Acts which followed the Boston Tea Party. In 1775 he was back in the Assembly.

JAMES SMITH, who was about fifty-seven years old and living at York, Pennsylvania, was born in northern Ireland, like George Taylor, and was also engaged in the iron business for a time, though without success. Primarily he was a lawyer and a representative of the back country. He came to America when about ten, received some schooling in Philadelphia, read law with an elder brother, and spent four or five years on the frontier in Cumberland County before settling at York. He was a leader in the struggle of the western counties against the eastern, and against British policy. In the years 1774–76 he was a member of successive provincial conferences and congresses; and he organized at York a militia company of which he was made captain, and, after it had grown in size, honorary colonel. In late July 1776, he was elected to the Continental Congress as a recognized supporter of independence.

He was in Congress until February 1777, and again from December of that year through 1778. He was not conspicuous, but his speeches were frequently enlivened by humor and he is said to have been an excellent storyteller. He held several state posts after leaving Congress and was re-elected to that body in 1785, declining

on account of age. He lived nearly a score of years longer, dying in 1806 when about eighty-seven. He long continued in the practice of law, being very successful, and no doubt a much fuller story of him could be told if his papers had not been destroyed by fire. He married Eleanor Armor of New Castle, Delaware, and they had five children. He was buried in the cemetery of the English Presbyterian Church in York.

Smith's burial place.

GEORGE ROSS, aged forty-six, was a lawyer, living in Lancaster and noted for his wit and good humor. Born in New Castle, Delaware, of Scottish stock, he was the son of an Anglican clergyman and seems to have been well educated by the standards of the time. After reading law in Philadelphia he was very successful in practice in Lancaster. For seven or eight years he was a member of the provincial Assembly, and in 1774 he served in the first Continental Congress, being then Loyalist in his sympathies and opinions. He turned to the Patriot side in 1775, was active in the Pennsylvania constitutional convention of 1776, helping draw the declaration of rights, and was one of the new delegates elected to Congress in late

July. His personal popularity is suggested by the fact that only Franklin got a larger vote than he in the balloting in the convention, but in Congress he did nothing memorable except to sign the Declaration. He is said to have disliked congressional business and, despite his attractive personality, he was not particularly influential during his brief stay.

Withdrawing early in 1777 because of illness, he afterward became a judge of the admiralty court of his state and presided over the celebrated case of Gideon Olmsted. Olmsted, a citizen of Connecticut, seized possession of the British sloop *Active* while serving as a captive on that vessel, but she was escorted into port by a brig belonging to the Commonwealth of Pennsylvania. The dispute was over the distribution of the prize money. A Pennsylvania jury awarded only a fourth to Olmsted and his associates, and three-fourths to the state. Ross, though sympathetic with Olmsted, saw no choice but to affirm the verdict, and when it was overruled by the court of appeals estab-

Mrs. George Ross.

The home of George Ross, Lancaster.

174

lished by Congress he denied the power of that body to take such action. Questions of state rights were involved and the legal controversy was not settled until a generation later, when the United States Supreme Court ruled for Olmsted.

Ross died very early in the controversy—in 1779 at the age of forty-nine. His death resulted from a violent attack of gout, and the implications are that he had enjoyed good living. He was buried in Christ Churchyard, Philadelphia. He had married Anne Lawler, a lady of Scots-Irish descent whose portrait by Benjamin West adorns these pages, and they had two sons and a daughter. Though his relatively brief career was marked by controversy at the very end, it seems generally to have been a merry one.

GEORGE CLYMER, who was thirty-seven years old at the time, fulfilled 'his dearest wish' when he signed the Declaration. Then a prosperous merchant in Philadelphia, where he was born, he had been orphaned while a very small child and brought up by a merchant uncle, William Coleman. He became a member of the firm of Merediths & Clymer, married the daughter of his senior partner, and in his father-in-law's house met George Washington, with whom he formed a lasting friendship. A modest man and cool on the surface, Clymer never sought public office, but for a score of years he was in almost unbroken public service, showing consistent republicanism and unusual warmth of devotion. An active Patriot from his very young manhood, he was one of the five elected to Congress from Pennsylvania for the first time in July 1776. While no orator, this handsome man was well informed, a witty conversationalist, and a good writer. It is a sign of his patriotism, though not of his

This tablet notes that Clymer signed the Constitution but not that he signed the Declaration.

worldly wisdom, that in 1776 he exchanged all his specie for Continental currency. In Congress, however, he was noted for his good sense as well as his great industry.

He served three or four years there, in three different stretches. With Richard Stockton he inspected the northern army at Ticonderoga in 1776; he was a member of the boards of war and of the treasury; and his report on a mission to Fort Pitt in 1777-78 led Congress to organize an expedition against Detroit. In the Penn-

sylvania Assembly, a little later, he advocated reforms in the penal code and the public employment of convicts. As a delegate to the Federal Convention in 1787, he was effective without being particularly vocal, and he signed the Constitution. As a member of the first Congress under the Constitution, he remained loyal to his friend Washington, but tended to side with Madison against Hamilton. After he declined re-election, he was appointed by Washington as head of the excise tax department for Pennsylvania. He found this office distasteful and resigned after his son Meredith, who was in the army dispatched against the Whiskey Rebels in 1794, died in Pittsburgh. In 1796 he performed his last public service as commissioner to the Cherokee and Creek Indians in Georgia, negotiating a treaty with them.

He lived until 1813 and was nearly seventy-four when he died in Morrisville, Pennsylvania. By his marriage with Elizabeth Meredith he had nine children, of whom five survived infancy. He was buried in the Friends Graveyard, Trenton, New Jersey, but the tablet at his grave, while referring to him as a signer of the Constitution, fails to mention the Declaration of Independence.

The Clymer house, Philadelphia.

177

BENJAMIN RUSH *became the most famous American physician and medical teacher of his time.*

BENJAMIN RUSH, in his thirty-first year, was the youngest of the Signers from Pennsylvania and one of the very youngest men in Congress. Also, he was one of the most versatile and vivacious. Born near Philadelphia, he graduated from the College of New Jersey (Princeton), began the study of medicine in Philadelphia, completed it in Edinburgh and London, and became the most famous American physician and medical teacher of his generation. In Philadelphia he was associated throughout most of his professional life with the Pennsylvania Hospital and the University of Pennsylvania, and he was a leading light of the American Philosophical Society. Like Franklin and Jefferson, he was interested in everything, and he passed his days 'like an arrow shot from a bow.'

He manifested his enthusiasm for the colonial cause by riding out to meet the Massachusetts delegates to the first Continental Congress in 1774, and he established during the next few years the deepest and most cherished of his friendships with public men—that with John Adams. He himself was elected to Congress in July 1776 after the Declaration had been adopted, but there was probably no one who signed the engrossed document with greater satisfaction. In Congress he found Richard Stockton of New Jersey, whose daughter Julia he had married early in the year, and President John Witherspoon, who had come to Princeton partly because of Rush's persuasion and who had performed the wedding ceremony. Also, he began a friendship with Thomas Jefferson second in significance only to that with John Adams.

After some months in Congress he became (April 1777) surgeon general of the armies of the Middle Department, but he resigned after less than a year when Congress failed to support him in a controversy over the administration of the military hospitals. Rush, who once described prudence as a 'rascally virtue'—of which he himself had little—was led into indiscreet remarks about Washington which seemed to involve him in the cabal against the General and these have served to cloud his fame to some extent until our own time. Impulsiveness and indiscretion were characteristic of him, but his zeal for the public good was limitless and, as a physician and public man, he threw himself into the task of transforming society according to republican principles. He attacked slavery and strong drink, classical education and tobacco, carrying on a 'one-man crusade' and undoubtedly spending himself in too many causes. He was the hero of the yellow-fever epidemic of 1793 in Philadelphia, though William Cobbett criticized—not without reason—his practice of bloodletting. Rush never wholly convinced his scientific friend Jefferson that the doctors of that time did more good than ill.

He went through a relatively conservative political phase after the Revolution, aiding James Wilson in connection with the Pennsylvania constitution of 1790, after having strongly supported the new Federal Constitution of 1787. In the partisan struggles of the 1790's, however, he was a Jeffersonian, while maintaining his close friendship with Adams. The latter magnanimously appointed him treasurer of the United States Mint, and he held this

Julia Stockton Rush was married before her seventeenth birthday.

position for sixteen years, despite his manifold professional activities. It was to Rush that Jefferson wrote privately, in the hot election year 1800, 'I have sworn upon the altar of God eternal hostility against every form of tyranny over the mind of man'; and, toward the end of his own life, the Doctor, as the self-appointed intermediary between Jefferson and Adams, brought about the renewal of their correspondence.

Rush's own correspondence remained unpublished for the most part until the middle of the twentieth century—chiefly because his family did not want to advertise old indiscretions and revive old controversies. This was unfortunate, since it did Rush himself an injustice. He was a prolific and vivid letter writer, and his correspondence is a mine of social and scientific history and biographical allusion. He also left in manuscript certain autobiographical writings which have recently been printed. These include brief accounts of the Revolutionary Patriots. His comment on himself consists of three words: 'He aimed well.'

He was at the height of his fame in 1813 when he died in Philadelphia in his sixty-eighth year. His beloved wife, Julia, who was not yet seventeen when he married her, bore him thirteen children. Two of them gained enduring distinction: Richard Rush, the diplomat; and James Rush, who followed his father in the medical profession. Thomas Sully's portrait of Benjamin Rush was painted toward the end of his life and, as his editor says, it shows him as a 'sweetly pensive old man,' giving no suggestion of his pugnacity and vivacity. It was just about this time that one of his many adoring pupils said that he looked like 'an angel of light,' and deserved deification if any mortal did. Without being at all sanctimonious, he had spent himself for the good of mankind throughout an extraordinarily full life, and we can see him now as one of the most colorful figures in a glorious generation.

Drawn Engraved & Published by W. Birch & Son   Sold by R. Campbell & Co. No. 30. Chesnut Street Philad.a 1799

PENNSYLVANIA HOSPITAL, in Pine Street PHILADELPHIA.

180

Rush was the founder of Pennsylvania Hospital, Philadelphia.

The vote of Delaware for the resolution of independence was cast under dramatic circumstances—because of the overnight ride of Caesar Rodney through the storm to get to Philadelphia in time. His voice, with that of Thomas McKean, gave a majority within the delegation to the advocates of immediate action; and George Read, who was in the minority at this point, accepted the decision and afterward signed the Declaration. There was a special flavor of local patriotism in the conduct of the leaders of Delaware, for the Three Lower Counties were separating themselves not only from the British Empire but also from Pennsylvania. Hitherto, while enjoying a separate legislative body, they had the same governor as Pennsylvania and had resented being regarded an appendage of the larger province. The little commonwealth, which was set up in 1776, afterward gained the historic distinction of being the first state to ratify the Constitution.

CAESAR RODNEY, who was in his forty-eighth year when he rode through the night and the rain from his home near Dover to vote for the resolution of independence, was a recognized leader in the movement to separate the Three Lower Counties from British rule. Born near Dover in Kent County, the grandson of an Anglican clergyman on the maternal side and the son of a planter, who died before his boy was grown, Rodney appears to have gained most of his education at home, as was so often the case with planters' sons. He entered public life early, as the custom also was, and for more than a dozen years before 1776 was almost continuously a member of the House of Assembly, serving during the last years as Speaker. Active in the militia, he became a brigadier general in 1775. He was a delegate to the first Continental Congress, and John Adams gave a vivid description of him the day he met him: 'Caesar Rodney is the oddest looking man in the world; he is tall, thin and slender as a reed, pale; his face is not bigger than a large apple, yet there is sense and fire, spirit, wit, and humor in his countenance.' The cancerous growth on his face, from which he suffered for years and finally died, may have contributed to the oddity of his appearance, but his actions showed him to be a man of heroic proportions.

His delay in getting to Congress in July 1776 was owing to the fact that, after presiding in June over the session of the Assembly or convention which authorized support of the intercolonial movement for independence and virtually declared Delaware independent of the Crown, he had gone to Sussex County to look into a threatened Loyalist uprising. He had just returned home when he learned from his colleague McKean that a vote was impending in

Congress, and he rushed northward to give his voice. The news of the Declaration was announced in Dover at a fine turtle feast, and a friend there soon congratulated him on 'the Important Day which restores to every American his birthright—a day which every freeman will record with gratitude, and millions of posterity will read with rapture.'

He had aroused conservative opposition in Kent County, however. During his continued absence in Congress this prevented his being elected to the state constitutional convention, and in the winter he was not even returned to Congress. He became active, therefore, in military affairs. He dispatched militia to Washington's army, and for a time he was in command of the post at Trenton. He again served briefly in Congress, after a bit, but his remaining public services were chiefly in his own state. He was appointed major general of militia by his friend Thomas McKean, then act-

ing as President of Delaware, and in 1778 he himself became President, as the chief executive of the state was then called. Serving until 1781, he was the war governor during a large part of the Revolution. His declining health interfered with later public service, but he was Speaker of the upper house of the legislature when he died in 1784 in his fifty-sixth year.

He never married and he left most of his estate to his nephew, Caesar Augustus Rodney, the son of his brother Thomas, who was also a prominent Patriot and public man. The nephew later became Attorney General of the United States. The Signer was buried on his home farm, but after a century his remains were removed to the Christ Episcopal Churchyard in Dover, and a few years later a monument to him was erected there. The equestrian statue in Wilmington was unveiled in 1923. A few years later he took his place in Statuary Hall in the Capitol in Washington.

Rodney, booted and spurred, votes for Independence.

183

184

GEORGE READ *opposed adoption of the Declaration; afterward signed and supported it.*

GEORGE READ, who was in his forty-third year in the summer of 1776 and lived in New Castle, Delaware, was born in Cecil County, Maryland. His father had been born in Dublin and his mother was Welsh. He read law in Philadelphia and practiced there for a time, and he was a close friend of John Dickinson. For a dozen years before the Declaration he was a member of the House of Assembly of the Three Lower Counties, and he served in both the first Continental Congress and the second. One of his colleagues described him as a shrewd lawyer, with gentle manners and considerable talent and knowledge, firm without being violent. More moderate and cautious than Caesar Rodney, he opposed the Declaration at the time it was adopted but afterward signed and strongly supported it. He was a tall, thin man, with fine features, and was rather austere in manner.

He was the presiding officer at the state constitutional convention of 1776 and had a large share in the constitution then adopted. At this stage he was the most influential man in Delaware. He served as President of the state for a time before Rodney, but he was less active in the latter part of the Revolution because of ill health. He was a delegate to both the Annapolis Convention of 1786 and the Federal Convention of 1787, favoring a strong national government to control the large states. He played the leading part in the ratification of the Constitution by Delaware, first among the states, and was United States Senator from the beginning of the new government until 1793, when he resigned to become chief justice of Delaware. He was regarded as a strong Federalist. He died in 1798 at New Castle, where his mansion commanded a fine river view.

He had married Gertrude Ross of New Castle, widow of Thomas Till and the daughter of an Episcopal clergyman. Among his five children was John Read, who became a prominent Philadelphia lawyer and Episcopal layman. His grandson, John Meredith Read, was an even more distinguished lawyer, and his great-grandson of the same name achieved distinction as a diplomat.

THOMAS MCKEAN at forty-two was the youngest of the Signers from Delaware, but he lived longer than the others and became the most conspicuous public man and the most controversial figure of the three. At this time he was living at New Castle, but he had legal practice not only in the Lower Counties but in New Jersey and Pennsylvania as well, and in the later phases of his career he was identified with the Keystone State.

Born in New London Township, Chester County, Pennsylvania, he came of Scots-Irish stock and was a man of vigorous personality. In Delaware, where he read law and had important family connections, he was a perennial member of the Assembly from his young manhood, and he became noted as a champion of the colonial cause against the British. Except for a period of about a year he represented Delaware in the Continental Congress continuously from 1774 to 1783, and it was his summons that caused Caesar Rodney to ride hurriedly to Philadelphia to join his vote with McKean's and carry the delegation for independence on July 2, 1776. There is considerable question about the time at which McKean

signed the Declaration. He certainly did not do this in August, and although he claimed in old age that he attached his name some time in 1776 it did not appear on the printed copy that was authenticated on January 17, 1777, and it is assumed that he signed after that date.

The Delaware constitution of 1776 has been credited to him as well as to George Read, and for a short time he was acting president of Delaware. His career is confusing because he held office in two commonwealths at the same time. Appointed chief justice of Pennsylvania in 1777, he occupied that post for twenty-two years, and as time went on he became increasingly identified with that state. He had been regarded as a radical Whig, but he opposed the Pennsylvania constitution of 1776, which Franklin approved, and was active in the convention that adopted the more conservative document of 1790. He strongly supported the new Federal Constitution, but in the party struggles of the 1790's he became a Republican against the Federalists.

His election as governor of Pennsylvania in 1799 was an important political event, and he served three terms of three years each in that

187

THOMAS McKEAN, *with his son, Thomas, Jr.*

Mrs. Thomas McKean and daughter Sophia Dorothea.

office. His policy of proscribing political opponents was sharply criticized, and he was eventually charged with nepotism. Though a representative of moderate rather than radical republicanism, he was generally a storm center. Part of his difficulties arose from his personality. This tall and stately man of unquestionable ability and honesty was cold in manner, vain, and tactless and he gained a host of enemies as well as admirers. He amassed a very considerable estate and gave evidence of his learning in the *Acts of the General Assembly of Pennsylvania,* which he edited, and in other writings.

After his retirement, he remained an impressive figure in Philadelphia until his death in 1817 at the age of eighty-three. His first wife, Mary Borden, the daughter of Joseph Borden of Bordentown, New Jersey, and sister of the wife of Francis Hopkinson, bore him six children; and his second wife, Sarah Armitage of New Castle, Delaware, bore him five. While governor he appointed his son, Joseph Borden McKean, as attorney general, and this action aroused gibes about the 'heir apparent' and 'royal family.' This son was a lawyer of ability, however, and he afterward held high judicial office.

Charles Carroll of Carrollton

Wm Paca   Samuel Chase

Thos Stone

The four Signers from Maryland averaged only a little more than thirty-five years in age, but their average wealth was very high because of the presence among them of Charles Carroll of Carrollton. To the New Englanders in this Congress and later ones the Marylanders seemed a pleasure-loving lot, with insufficient respect for good honest labor. A more sympathetic observer described colonial Annapolis as the 'most genteel' place in North America; and, except for the boisterous and belligerent Samuel Chase, the members of this little group were notable for good manners. At the same time, these gentlemen were notably devoted to the cause of independence. On this important point sentiment in the Chesapeake Bay country, unlike that in the middle provinces, seemed practically undivided.

189

CHARLES CARROLL OF CARROLLTON, in his thirty-ninth year, was often described as the richest man in the country and was the only Catholic among the Signers. A colleague estimated his estate as being worth £200,000 sterling, and it would not be an exaggeration to term him a millionaire. The designation, 'of Carrollton,' dates back to his early manhood when his father settled on him the Manor of Carrollton, comprising some 10,000 acres in Frederick County, Maryland; and its purpose was to distinguish him from others of the same name—including his father, Charles Carroll of Annapolis. He himself was the third Charles in America in the direct line, and the same Chris-

tian name was borne by a contemporary kinsman with whom he is sometimes confused. The Signer himself was born in genteel Annapolis and he was much more likely to be found in his father's brick town house or in the favorite country seat of the family, 'Doughoregan,' than at 'Carrollton.' The Carrolls were Irish, the name having originally been O'Carroll, and they traced their line back to Irish kings. The latter were so plentiful at one time that they might be better described as princes or heads of clans, but few American families had a more indisputable background of aristocracy in the Old World or could be more accurately described as aristocratic in the New.

Doughoregan, near Ellicott City, was the favorite country seat of the Carrolls.

The first of the line in America, Charles the Attorney General, enjoyed the favor of Lord Baltimore, the Catholic Proprietor of Maryland, when he came in 1688, but the political authority of his patron was temporarily destroyed by the Revolution of that year in England and Carroll found Maryland no haven of religious freedom. He received large grants of land from the Proprietor, however, and laid firm foundations for the vast fortune of his family. His grandson, the Signer, was born in Annapolis and educated in his early years by Jesuits. He then spent many years in school in Europe. His long stay in French-speaking countries enabled him to become fluent in that language, and there was a distinct flavor of foreign elegance about him when he returned to Maryland at the age of twenty-eight. He had studied law in Paris and London and was an unusually cultivated as well as an exceedingly rich young man. Slight in stature, he was graceful in his movements and an accomplished horseman, and he had fine, regular features. At the age of thirty-one he married his cousin, Mary Darnall, known in the family as Molly, and he lived the life of a landed gentleman without entering into politics. As a Catholic he was subjected to political disabilities until the American Revolution set the Republic on the road of religious freedom.

Not until 1773, when he was thirty-six, did he become a public man. Then Daniel Dulany, defending the action of the proprietary Governor in setting by proclamation, without legislative sanction, the fees of civil officers and clergymen of the Established Church (Anglican), published a series of articles in which as a Second Citizen he answered the arguments of a First. Carroll, taking the popular side, countered Dulany very effectively and gained the title of 'First Citizen' as his own. From that time on he was recognized as a leading Patriot, though he performed most of his services unofficially. Early in 1776 he was sent by Congress, with Franklin and fellow-Marylander Samuel Chase, on what proved to be a vain mission to Canada. A main reason for his inclusion was that he was a Catholic, and he persuaded his kinsman John Carroll, afterward the first Roman Catholic bishop in the United States, to go along. It was after this mission that Charles Carroll was elected to Congress and signed the Declaration.

He remained in Congress for a couple of years, meanwhile playing an important part in the Maryland constitutional convention of 1776, from which emerged one of the more conservative state constitutions of the era. It was coupled with a Declaration of Rights, however, and from this time forward there was no established church in Maryland. Carroll also served in the upper house of the state legislature, but at no time was his prominence attributable to the relatively few public offices he held. He declined appointment as a delegate to the Federal Convention of 1787, though he supported the Constitution. For two years he was in the United States Senate but he withdrew to enter again the Maryland Senate, where he stayed longer. His political views at this stage were distinctly conservative.

He retired from public life in 1800 but lived until 1832, being the only surviving Signer when he died at the age of ninety-five. He had emerged to lay the cornerstone of the Baltimore and Ohio Railroad four years earlier. Still regarded as the richest man in the country, he had long been a legendary figure. He was buried at Doughoregan Manor, near Ellicott City. This favored child of fortune had graced the position he inherited and had enriched the American heritage by identifying himself, at a decisive moment, with the cause of freedom.

Carroll, who outlived all the other Signers, was buried in the chapel of Doughoregan Manor.

194

WILLIAM PACA, who was in his thirty-sixth year, came of a prosperous family, which may have been Italian, that for several generations had been established in Maryland. Born in Abingdon, Harford County, he received a master's degree from the College of Philadelphia, read law in Annapolis, and continued his legal studies at the Inner Temple. In 1776 he was practicing law in Annapolis and had long been one of the leading Patriots of the province. He was a member of the first Continental Congress and served in the second from 1775 to 1779. He was an effective committeeman, widely respected, and well liked. Dr. Rush, who liked him, thought him too indolent to exercise his excellent understanding fully, and believed that his talents were greater than his reputation would indicate.

After some judicial service he was elected governor of Maryland in 1782 and twice re-elected without opposition, serving three years altogether. Though not wholly satisfied with the Federal Constitution of 1787, he voted for its ratification in the state convention. Appointed in 1789 a United States district judge, he remained in this post until his death ten years later at the age of fifty-nine. He was buried at his country place, 'Wye Hall,' in Talbot County. Of his five children by his first wife, Mary Chew of Annapolis, only one attained maturity; and by his second wife, Anne Harrison of Philadelphia, he had no children. Though William Paca was relatively inconspicuous on the national stage, this able, public-spirited man commanded respect throughout his career.

Paca, who served three terms as governor of Maryland, lived in this house in Annapolis.

SAMUEL CHASE, thirty-five years old, was the biggest and most violent member of the Maryland delegation. Born in Somerset County, the son of an Anglican clergyman, he was educated in the classics by his father and read law in Annapolis, where he practiced and made his home until he moved to Baltimore in 1786. Entering public life soon after he was grown, he was regularly a member of the provincial Assembly, and from the very start he belonged to the faction opposing the proprietary governor. The most aggressive anti-British leader in Maryland, he was a delegate to the first Continental Congress and to the second. He was chiefly responsible for the action of the provincial convention in June 1776 in favor of independence, and, although his ride to Philadelphia with fresh instructions has been less publicized than that of Caesar Rodney, it was considerably longer.

He remained in Congress several years, but became discredited in 1778 when charged in the newspapers with taking advantage of inside information in order to deal in flour; he did not regain political prominence for a decade. Business enterprises into which he entered turned out badly, and in 1789 he was insolvent. Meanwhile, he had assumed judicial office in Baltimore, and he afterward became chief judge of the general court of Maryland in addition. All his actions were accompanied by considerable turmoil and he was criticized for holding so many offices. He had opposed the United States Constitution of 1787, but in the 1790's he became a pronounced Federalist, and in 1796 President Washington appointed him an associate justice of the Supreme Court.

He was not viewed very favorably by his colleagues at the time, and his career on the bench turned out to be one of the stormiest on record. He revealed his intellectual power in some of the most important of the pre-Marshall decisions, but his bullying tactics in certain of the sedition trials, and his use of the bench for partisan harangues against the Republicans, led to his impeachment during the Presidency of Jefferson. He deserved rebuke for his high-handed partisanship, but he had not been guilty of high crimes and misdemeanors within the constitutional framework, and he was acquitted. This outcome of a notorious case represented an obvious defeat for the administration, but henceforth the justices themselves showed better manners. Chase's judicial career was relatively unimportant from that time on, partly because of his sufferings from gout. He died in 1811 at the age of seventy and was buried in Baltimore. He was twice married: to

Chase's three-story home was an unusually large Annapolis house.

SAMUEL CHASE *was the most aggressive Patriot in Maryland.*

Mrs. Anne Chase and her daughters.

Anne Baldwin of Annapolis, who bore him two sons and two daughters; and to Hannah Kilty Giles, an Englishwoman by whom he had no children.

Because of his fiery complexion, Chase was given the name 'Bacon face' at the Maryland bar. No one can deny that his career was checkered. One of his colleagues in the Continental Congress said that he had 'more learning than knowledge, and more of both than judgment.' Justice Story gave a classic description of him in old age: 'His manners are coarse, and in appearance harsh; but in reality he abounds with good humor. . . In person, in manners, in unwieldly strength, in severity of reproof, in real tenderness of heart, and above all in intellect, he is the living, I had almost said the exact, image of Samuel Johnson.' He was an immense man disliked by some and liked hugely by others.

THOMAS STONE, aged thirty-three, was the youngest and quietest of the delegates from Maryland. Born in Charles County, he was the grandson of a proprietary governor. He read law in Annapolis, practiced in Frederick, and after his marriage to Margaret Brown moved back to Charles County, building (about 1771) 'Habre-de-Venture' and living there thenceforth. He entered Congress in 1775 and was a more moderate Patriot than his three fellow Signers of the Declaration, though he joined with them in voting for it. He was a tall, thin man but well-proportioned; he was also well-mannered.

Habre-de-Venture.

He served several years in Congress and in the upper house of the Maryland legislature but rarely spoke in either. What is known about him is creditable, but little can be written about him since his career was short and he left few records. He declined membership in the Federal Convention of 1787 because of the alarming state of his wife's health. She died in the middle of that year, and he in the autumn at the age of forty-four. They had three children. He is buried at 'Habre-de-Venture.'

200

Stone's grave at Habre-de-Venture.

Richard Henry Lee

Th Jefferson

Benj Harrison

George Wythe   Carter Braxton

Francis Lightfoot Lee   Th: Nelson jr.

201

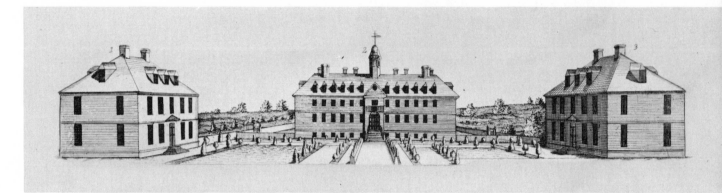

The College of William and Mary.

'These gentlemen from Virginia appear to be the most spirited and consistent of any,' said John Adams in the first Continental Congress and his comment was equally appropriate in the second. In later years he and his old friend Jefferson concurred in the opinion that independence was chiefly owing to the efforts of the New Englanders and the Virginians. They could not afford to say that in public and no exclusive claim can be justly made, but quite obviously these were the men who took the lead in 1776.

There were more Signers from Virginia than from any other state except Pennsylvania, and these seven men comprised an impressive and homogeneous group. All of them were in some sense planters; all were men of substance; all were in the prime of life. Jefferson was the youngest and seems to have been the tallest, though Richard Henry Lee also towered; and if Harrison and Nelson were not the fattest men in Congress they were among the fattest, being notably jovial to boot. No one of these men gained in his personal fortunes from the Revolution and some lost heavily. They were Patriots who took a large view of things.

RICHARD HENRY LEE, who was in his forty-fifth year when he introduced in Congress the famous resolutions that led to the Declaration, was the ranking, and most conspicuous, member of the delegation from Virginia. Tall and spare, with bold features, he was a noted orator, and was called Cicero, as Patrick Henry was Demosthenes, but he lacked the emotional appeal of his former colleague, who was not in Congress at this time. Lee was rather stilted in manner, and he was charged by a local contemporary with practicing his gestures before the mirror. He was particularly attractive to the New Englanders—more because of his views and his attitude toward them, probably, than his public manner. John Adams regarded him as 'masterly' and Samuel Adams established very close relations with him. He was not the most likable member of the delegation, but he had been one of the most aggressive of the Virginia Patriots, and at this stage his prominence was warranted.

Actually, he went home to share in the work of the Virginia convention some days before the crucial resolution of independence was adopted on July 2, but he will always be famous for having started it on its way.

Born at 'Stratford' in Westmoreland County, he belonged to one of the most distinguished of Virginia families. He received much of his education abroad and was trained for the public life which was assumed to be the portion of a prominent planter. Elected to the House of Burgesses as a matter of course, he became a prominent member, and in the long controversy with the mother country he was associated with the more aggressive faction, of which Patrick Henry was the spokesman, rather than with the more sedate and somewhat more patient older leaders. There were some inconsistencies in his record, however, and some people regarded him as a self-seeker.

The most glorious part of his career ended in 1776. When he returned to Congress he continued to manifest great interest in foreign affairs, and his concern for the establishment of the Confederation caused him to labor for the cession of Virginia's western lands. But he was involved in the bitter controversy between his brother Arthur and Silas Deane, who served together as commissioners in France, and as time went on he became very unpopular at home. During the latter part of the Revolution he was in Virginia and after the war he was again in Congress, where he was an effective member. He was one of the leading opponents of the Constitution of 1787, his *Letters of a Federal Farmer* serving as a sort of textbook of the opposition, but he failed of election to the Virginia ratifying convention. He was elected to the first United States Senate, but he resigned in 1792 because of ill health. He died two years later in his sixty-third year and was buried at his place, 'Chantilly,' not far from 'Stratford,' where Robert E. Lee, the most famous of the family, was born early in the next century. The General was descended from a cousin of Richard Henry's. The Signer had nine children by his two wives, Anne Aylett and Mrs. Anne Gaskins Pinckard. None of his sons achieved distinction, but in the Revolutionary era his three brothers did. These were Francis Lightfoot, William, and Arthur, and the first of them was also a Signer.

Stratford, Westmoreland County, Virginia.

THOMAS JEFFERSON, who was thirty-three when he wrote the Declaration, was the youngest of the Virginia delegates; nevertheless only Richard Henry Lee had received a larger vote than he in the election. By no means the richest of the Virginians, he had inherited from his father a considerable estate and an established position, and by his marriage he had doubled his holdings of land and slaves.

In the years 1774-76, when he took the road to political revolt, he was more prosperous than he was ever to be thereafter.

Born at 'Shadwell' in what is now Albemarle County, he received an excellent classical education at the hands of private teachers and attended the College of William and Mary, where his mind was opened to the delights of science. For five years he studied law under the direction of the most notable law teacher of his time and locality, George Wythe, and he improved himself by incessant reading. He had ceased the practice of law in 1774, when the courts were closed, and always he was chiefly supported by his own lands. A recognized member of the gentry of the province, he took more seriously than most the liberal and humane ideas of the eighteenth-century Enlightenment. He had begun his famous mansion, 'Monticello,' before he married, but the mansion that present-day visitors see was not completed until early in the nineteenth century, when he was President.

He was well over six feet in height, slim and erect, strong in body at this stage, and a noted horseman. Reddish-haired and inclined to freckle, he was never particularly prepossessing in appearance, but the familiar stories about his indifference to dress date from a later period. Though shy with strangers, he was notably amiable in personal relations. From his early manhood he participated actively in public life, as one in his position was expected to do. In the House of Burgesses, where he served continuously from the age of twenty-six, he made his mark as a draftsman, though not as a speaker. Properly regarded as an unswerving Patriot, he was sent to Congress in 1775 as a substitute for Peyton Randolph, who had been called home, but he now stood near the top of the delegation in his own right and at the very top as a penman.

The part that he played as draftsman of the Declaration has already been described. In his own judgment his services to the cause of human liberty in the legislature of Virginia, beginning in the autumn of 1776, were equally important. In the next three years he procured the abolition of entails, led the fight for the disestablishment of the Church, and, as a member of the Committee on Revisors, recommended far-reaching reforms in the legal code of the state. The abolition of primogeniture followed, and his Bill for Establishing Religious Freedom was eventually adopted, though his forward-looking proposals for public education were rejected. His governorship of two years, during a time of British invasion, ended unhappily, largely through fault of circumstances; and before he was forty he was plunged into deepest grief by the death of his wife. He had married Mrs. Martha Wayles Skelton only a little more than ten years before. Returning to public life to assuage his grief, he served impressively in Congress, spent five years in France as commercial commissioner and as minister, in succession to Franklin, and in 1790 became the first secretary of state under the new Constitution. Retiring from that office after three years, he was elected Vice President in 1796, and in 1801 he became President.

His career after the Revolution, like that of John Adams, is so integral a part of the history of the country that it cannot and need not be described here. The most important thing to

The Monticello of today was completed while Jefferson was President.

say is that the author of the Declaration throughout the rest of his life sought to apply to the changing problems of his time the ideas and ideals he had written into that famous document. The freedom of the individual human being was ever his main concern, and it was his faith in men that made him a prophet of progress. In his old age he fathered the University of Virginia, and he valued public enlightenment next after private freedom. His zeal for useful knowledge was richly manifested in his personal achievements in invention, agriculture, science, architecture, and linguistics and in lifelong patronage of learning in its every aspect. No other American public man of the first rank, except Franklin, ever matched him in versatility, and no one ever strove more incessantly to be useful.

Only two of his six children, both daughters, lived to grow up. Of these, Martha, who married Thomas Mann Randolph, later governor of Virginia, survived her father and has left numerous descendants. Mary, or Maria, Jefferson, who married John Wayles Eppes, afterward a congressman, died while her father was President and her descendants are less numerous than her sister's. Jefferson himself died, shortly before his fellow Signer, John Adams,

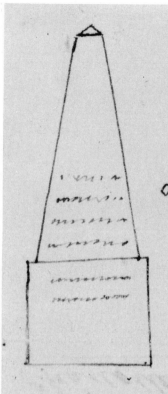

could the dead feel any interest in Monu-
-ments or other remembrances of them, when, as
Anacreon says: Ολίγη δε κεισομεσθα
        Κονις, οστεων λυθεντων
the following would be to my Manes the most
gratifying.
On the grave
        a plain die or cube of 3.f without any
mouldings, surmounted by an Obelisk
of 6.f. height, each of a single stone:
on the faces of the Obelisk the following
inscription, & not a word more
        Here was buried
        Thomas Jefferson
    Author of the Declaration of American Independance
        of the Statute of Virginia for religious freedom
    & Father of the University of Virginia.
because by these, as testimonials that I have lived, I wish most to
be remembered. ~~~~~~~ to be of the coarse stone of which
my columns are made, that no one might be tempted
hereafter to destroy it for the value of the materials.
my bust by Ciracchi, with the pedestal and truncated
column on which it stands, might be given to the University
if they would place it in the Dome room of the Rotunda.
on the Die, of the Obelisk might be engraved
        Born Apr. 2. 1743. O.S.
        Died ———   ,

208

Jefferson's instructions for his tombstone.

on July 4, 1826, at the age of eighty-three. He rode horseback until almost the end of his life, and in his last years carried on an incredibly extensive correspondence. His long life may be attributed to a strong native constitution and to his temperate habits.

Ever since the Revolution he had been harassed by debt, much of which can be attributed to the inflation of that era. During his retirement his hospitality was costly, and in the troubles that befell most landed Virginians after the War of 1812 his situation became distressed. Finally, he stood surety too generously for a friend, and the result was his virtual bankruptcy at the very end. He was buried at his beloved 'Monticello,' beside his adored wife and deeply mourned younger daughter, and through the years countless thousands have seen his tombstone on the hillside. On it the Declaration is listed first among his memorable achievements. He symbolizes, as no other historic American does, the idea of freedom, while the rich record of his own life shows how freedom can be coupled with responsibility.

Jefferson's tombstone.

BENJAMIN HARRISON, aged fifty, was chairman of the committee of the whole and presided over the debates on the Declaration. A man of huge frame and florid face, he has been described as the Falstaff of the Congress, but through long participation in public business he had become well acquainted with it and he presided with firmness and dignity.

Born at 'Berkeley' in Charles City County, Virginia, he was the fifth Benjamin Harrison in direct line, and to distinguish him from the others he is designated as 'the Signer.' He was also a grandson of the fabulous 'King' Carter and a first cousin of Carter Braxton, another Signer from Virginia. The initials of his father and mother are in the brickwork at 'Berkeley,' which was built a half century before the Declaration and is still a showplace. Thomas Jefferson, who often visited the place, spelled the name 'Barclay,' thus suggesting the contemporary pronunciation of it. Harrison attended the College of William and Mary, and, as a planter and member of a prominent family, he was elected to the House of Burgesses at an early age, according to the custom. He served there continuously for a quarter of a century and frequently was Speaker.

While unwilling to go quite as far as Patrick Henry in protesting against the Stamp Act, he was a robust champion of colonial rights and was chosen as a delegate to the first Continental Congress. He said that he would have gone to Philadelphia on foot if necessary, and this was a striking expression of zeal on the part of a portly representative of a society in which nobody ever walked. The later aspersions of John Adams on him as 'an indolent, luxurious, heavy gentleman,' who was useless in Congress, may be attributed, perhaps, to Harrison's dislike of the 'leading characters' from New England and his strong local patriotism. There is no possible doubt of his conviviality and love for joking, but he served effectively on many important committees during his three or four years in Congress and played a significant part in the organization of the government.

Leaving the Continental legislature in 1778, he was for three years Speaker of the Virginia House of Delegates, and afterward was for three years Governor. In the state ratifying convention, he urged the inclusion of a bill of rights in the new Federal Constitution before rather than after the adoption of that document. He was back in the state legislature when he died in 1791 at the age of sixty-five. For forty years this scion of a great landed family had been a public man. He married Elizabeth Bassett and had seven children who survived infancy. Among these was William Henry Harrison, later President of the United States. The Signer had other distinguished descendants, including President Benjamin Harrison.

Harrison was born at Berkeley. It was plundered by Benedict Arnold during the Revolution.

GEORGE WYTHE, who like Benjamin Harrison was fifty, was one of the two oldest members of the Virginia delegation. (His name is pronounced so as to rhyme with Smith.) A leading legal light, he was a man of such unassuming character that he was often regarded as a follower rather than a leader in the long conflict with the mother country, but at all times he was in the forefront as a thinker. Nobody grasped better than he the essence of the constitutional struggle and the significance of these revolutionary events in the history of human freedom.

Born in Elizabeth County, Virginia, on the plantation of his father, who died intestate a few years later, he was left in rather straitened circumstances, since the estate descended to an elder brother according to the law of primogeniture. Taught largely by his unusual mother, who was of Quaker stock, and by himself, he gained a notable mastery of Latin and Greek. Throughout his career he sprinkled his speeches, legal opinions, and letters with classical quotations; and it was said that 'he could hardly refrain from giving a line from Horace the force of an act of Assembly.' He attended the College of William and Mary, presumably in the grammar school, and read law with an uncle, who seems to have treated him more like a clerk than a student. Admitted to the bar about the time he became grown, he practiced for seven or eight years in Spotsylvania County, but his career did not really get started until he was about thirty, when he was established in Williamsburg and had come into an inheritance after his brother's death. His first wife, Ann Lewis, had died after about a year; his second was Elizabeth Taliaferro (pronounced 'Tolliver'), whose father built the dignified house on the Palace Green they occupied for many years before it became legally theirs by will. The Wythe House is viewed day after day by thousands of visitors to restored Williamsburg.

He had already become a leader of the Virginia bar when Jefferson came to the colonial capital and began to study law under his wise guidance. Wythe was intimate with Governor Francis Fauquier and Dr. William Small, who taught mathematics and natural philosophy at the College of William and Mary, and for a score of years before the Revolution he was a member of the House of Burgesses, long serving as clerk of that body. His championship of colonial rights was as unquestionable as his devotion to the liberal and humane philosophy of the eighteenth-century Enlightenment, and it would have been little short of tragic if he had been denied the opportunity to vote for the Declaration and sign it.

One of his fellow Signers from another state said that he had seldom known a man with 'more modesty, or a more dove-like simplicity

213

Wythe, who lived in this house in Williamsburg, was the first professor of law in an American institution of higher learning.

and gentleness of manner.' These qualities were probably a disadvantage to him as an advocate; and, appropriately enough, his most memorable achievements were as a legal scholar, a judge, and a teacher. With Jefferson and Edmund Pendleton he was a reviser of the laws of Virginia, and in 1778 he became a judge in the new high court of chancery. He was Chancellor Wythe for the rest of his life, much of the time as sole chancellor. Meanwhile, he had assumed at the College of William and Mary in 1779 the first professorship of law in an American institution of higher learning. He held this until 1790, and in later years when his judicial duties caused him to reside in Richmond, he had a law school there. Of his eminent law students, Jefferson worked with him longest; John Marshall and Henry Clay studied with him briefly.

The death of this learned, liberal, and winsome man was caused by the drinking of coffee which his grandnephew, the chief beneficiary under his will, had poisoned with arsenic. The Chancellor, eighty years old and probably senile at the time (1806), was childless. He was notoriously kind to his slaves and emancipated all of them by will. He left his books to his friend President Jefferson. As he grew old he wrote his letters in large, childish script, but in them he unfailingly included Greek and Latin phrases. He is buried in St. John's Churchyard, Richmond.

FRANCIS LIGHTFOOT LEE, the younger brother of Richard Henry Lee, was in his forty-second year. Regarded by many as fully the equal of his brother and by some as his superior, he rarely if ever spoke in Congress and thus was overshadowed. Also born at 'Stratford' in Westmoreland County, he was a planter, making his home at 'Menokin' in Richmond County. His mansion is in a state of decrepitude, but even in its heyday it was not comparable with the more famous Virginia places. He was a member of the House of Burgesses continuously from the age of twenty-four, and was regarded as an even more ardent Patriot than his brother.

FRANCIS LIGHTFOOT LEE.

He was not a member of the Virginia delegation of 1775 as originally elected, but was added when Richard Bland asked to be relieved because of the infirmities of age. He remained in Congress until 1779, being effective on committees though silent during debate. For a time thereafter he was a member of the Virginia legislature, but he soon retired to the quietude of country life. He differed from his brother Richard Henry in strongly favoring the new Federal Constitution. He died early in 1797 in his sixty-third year and was buried on his own plantation. He had married Rebecca Tayloe but they had no children.

215

Lee's old home, Menokin, fell to rack and ruin.

CARTER BRAXTON, now in his fortieth year, was probably the most reluctant of the Virginia delegates in supporting the cause of independence. He was also one of those who suffered most in his own fortunes as a result of the war. Born at Newington in King and Queen County, he was the son of a wealthy planter and the grandson, on his mother's side, of 'King' Carter. He attended the College of William and Mary, married early, and after the death of his young wife spent several years in England. He was afterward charged with retaining 'British prejudices.' In 1776 he was a planter in King William County, which he long

represented in the House of Burgesses. His brick mansion, 'Elsing Green,' overlooking the Pamunkey River, has his initials in a plaque in the walls, but is said to have been built in 1758 by his brother while Carter Braxton was abroad.

Though his opposition to British policy during the years of controversy was more moderate than that of Patrick Henry, the Lees, and Jefferson, he signed the important patriotic agreements and was a member of the successive revolutionary conventions in Virginia. He was elected to the Continental Congress to fill a vacancy, taking his seat in February 1776. His failure of re-election in the late summer of that year, when the size of the delegation was reduced from seven to five, has been attributed to the conservative stand he took on the new Virginia constitution. He was a member of the General Assembly nearly all the rest of his life, and, while skeptical of popular government, he showed liberality of spirit when he supported Jefferson's famous Bill for Establishing Religious Freedom.

The loss of his cargoes during the war and the failure of many of his own debtors involved him in financial difficulties in his later years. During the final decade of his life he made his home in Richmond, dying there in 1797 at the age of sixty-one. He was twice married—to Judith Robinson and Elizabeth Corbin—and had sixteen children, though only ten of these survived infancy.

Elsing Green, Braxton's spacious home, overlooked the Pamunkey River.

Thomas Nelson, Jr., sat for his portrait while a boy.

THOMAS NELSON, Jr., thirty-seven years old, was the youngest of the Virginia delegates except Jefferson. He was described about this time by John Adams as a fat man, though 'alert and lively for his weight.' Nothing ponderous is suggested by the charming portrait of him as a boy, but this aristocratic gentleman had undoubtedly lived well all his life. He was the grandson of Thomas Nelson of Yorktown, known as 'Scotch Tom,' the merchant-planter who was the American founder of one of the wealthiest of Virginia families; and he was the son of William Nelson, long a member of the Council and at one time acting Governor of the Province, who was generally known as 'President Nelson.'

The Signer, as Thomas Nelson, Jr., is called to distinguish him from an uncle of the same name (known as Secretary Nelson), was born at Yorktown, attended private school in England, and was for several years at Cambridge. His English education did not at all incline him toward Loyalism, however. Returning to Virginia, he became a member of the Council at the age of twenty-six, and he knew Jefferson well while the latter was a student in Williamsburg. Rebecca Burwell, for whom young Jefferson sighed in vain, was President Nelson's ward, and his intimate friend John Page came of a family closely allied with the Nelsons. The famous Nelson House at Yorktown, where Page and Jefferson often visited, was built by either 'Scotch Tom' or the Signer's father. In its lines it is much like Benjamin Harrison's 'Berkeley,' though richer in its details. In their strategic location at Yorktown, the Nelsons were great merchants as well as great planters. Though conservative on economic and social questions, they were staunch Patriots. The Signer resigned his commission as Colonel in the militia to attend the second Continental Congress; and in May 1776 he bore to Philadelphia the resolutions of the Virginia convention which precipitated the action of Richard Henry Lee in Congress. This large and wealthy man played an important part in the movement for independence.

Leaving Congress in the spring of 1777, Nelson performed his chief services thereafter in the military sphere. As Brigadier General, he

The Nelson house, Yorktown.

*Nelson is said to have directed American fire at his own home,
occupied by Cornwallis, during the final siege of Yorktown.*

commanded the militia of his state; and in 1781,
succeeding his friend Jefferson as governor when
the state was overrun with British invaders, he
was for some months practically the military
dictator of Virginia. He himself was engaged
in the final siege of Yorktown; and, according
to tradition, he urged General Washington to
fire on his own home, the Nelson House, where
Cornwallis had his headquarters.

Both Nelson's health and fortunes were
wrecked by the war, and he removed with his
large family to a small estate in Hanover
County. There he died of asthma in 1789, a
week after he became sixty. He had married
Lucy Grymes and they had eleven children.
The fifth of these, Hugh Nelson, who later
made his home in Albemarle County, gained
distinction as a jurist and diplomat and was
prominent in the affairs of the Episcopal
Church. Thomas Jefferson Page and Thomas
Nelson Page were direct descendants of the
Signer.

Joseph Hewes,   *John Penn*

Wm Hooper

North Carolina had a certain primacy in the movement that led to the Declaration of Independence, for the provincial congress there authorized the delegates in Congress from this colony to vote for independence before the Virginia convention of 1776 had acted. We do not consider here the controversial Mecklenburg Declaration of the previous year, since that did not enter into the main current of events, but it also suggests the fervor of the Patriots of North Carolina.

By odd circumstance, all three of the Signers from the Old North State were born outside of its borders. Two of them were lawyers, one was a prosperous merchant, and all three died before reaching the age of fifty. They served chiefly in the early stages of the Revolution and won their places in history almost entirely from their connection with the Declaration.

JOSEPH HEWES, at forty-six years, was the oldest member of the North Carolina delegation and one of the most indefatigable workers in Congress, though an infrequent speaker. Born in Kingston, New Jersey, of Quaker stock, he engaged successfully in commerce in Philadelphia and removed in his late twenties to Edenton, North Carolina, the shipping center of the Albemarle Sound district. There he prospered as a merchant and became a greatly be-

loved and respected figure. Though he slipped out of the Quaker fold, he remained a plain and peaceful man. Beginning in 1766, he was regularly a member of the provincial Assembly, and he was active in every phase of the movement in North Carolina to protect colonial rights. In 1774 he was sent to the first Continental Congress.

In 1776, laboring incessantly in the second Congress, he did not leave Philadelphia to at-

*A monument on the courthouse green
at Edenton to the memory of Hewes.*

tend the provincial congress in North Carolina in April. It was at this meeting that the delegates in the Continental Congress were empowered to vote for 'independency.' Hewes had been reluctant to come to an open breach with the mother country, despite his ardent colonial patriotism, and this friendly man had resented the recriminations which were rife in Congress in the spring. Advice about the state of opinion in his own province caused him to shift his position to the side of independence, and John Adams regarded this as a highly important decision at the time. He supported the resolution of Richard Henry Lee in June, and he and his colleague John Penn voted for it in July, William Hooper then being absent.

During his stay in Congress until 1777, when he failed of re-election, he performed his most important service as chairman of the marine committee, where his knowledge of shipping stood him in good stead, and he was virtually the first head of the United States Navy. He knew John Paul Jones and was responsible for getting him a ship. After serving in the legislature of North Carolina, Hewes returned to Congress in 1779, but he died that year, presumably from overwork.

His fiancée in North Carolina had died years before, and he had never married. He was buried in Christ Churchyard, Philadelphia, but afterward, most appropriately, a monument was erected to him in old Edenton.

This little-known picture of John Penn was painted by Charles Willson Peale.

JOHN PENN, thirty-six years old in 1776, had moved to North Carolina only two years earlier from the neighboring province of Virginia, where he was born in Caroline County and had read law in the library of his distinguished kinsman, Edmund Pendleton. He was living and practicing law in Williamsboro, Granville County, North Carolina, at the time. Contemporary comments describe him as goodhumored, and he was a very popular man. He became a local leader in the patriotic cause, serving in the provincial congress in 1775 and then being elected to the Continental Congress.

He returned to North Carolina in the spring of 1776 to attend the provincial congress that authorized support of independence. He was particularly impressed by Thomas Paine's pamphlet, *Common Sense,* and appears to have been in advance of his colleagues Hewes and Hooper in advocating a complete break with the mother country. He voted for Lee's resolution and duly signed the Declaration.

It was said that Penn, though very talkative in private, rarely spoke in Congress except to whisper to the man next to him. During his tenure (1775-1777, 1778-1780) he was, however, very diligent in public business. Afterward he was a member of the board of war in his own state, but he virtually retired from public life in 1781 because of the state of his health, and he died in 1788 at the age of forty-eight. He married Susannah Lyme and had three children. He was buried on his own estate, but a century later his remains were reinterred at Guilford Battleground, where a monument to him and William Hooper now stands.

Penn's home near Stovall, North Carolina.

WILLIAM HOOPER, at thirty-four the youngest of the Signers from North Carolina, was born in Boston, the son of a Congregational minister, and was a graduate of Harvard College. After studying law with James Otis and perhaps imbibing some of that brilliant advocate's zeal for colonial rights, he removed to North Carolina in his early twenties. He established himself in the practice of law in Wilmington and married into the gentry of the Cape Fear district in the southern part of the province. As deputy attorney general and as a member of Governor Tryon's expedition which put down the Regulators in the western Carolinas, he was conspicuously opposed to that movement against eastern rule. The embittered frontiers-

men afterward tended to be Loyalists, hating the British less than they did the easterners, with whom Hooper was definitely associated. As a Patriot he was not a 'popular' leader, and the later decline in his political fortunes may be attributed in part to the growing power of the more 'democratic' elements, with which he was unsympathetic.

After serving in the provincial Assembly he was elected to the first Continental Congress in 1774, as he was to the second in the next year. A man of great personal attractiveness, as his portrait suggests, and of genuine cultivation, he was rated by John Adams as one of the leading orators. Dr. Rush, with more restraint, described him as a sprightly and sensible young

Hooper, originally buried in Hillsboro, was reburied in Guilford
Courthouse National Military Park. Penn was reburied here, too.

lawyer, and a rapid but correct speaker. He was absent when the vote on independence was taken, signing the Declaration after his return later in the summer. He remained in Congress until the following spring, when he returned to North Carolina to recoup his personal fortunes. He was in the state legislature for five years thereafter.

His property was greatly injured and his family endangered when the British captured Wilmington, and he afterward removed to Hillsboro. He remained to some extent in public life but never regained his early prominence. Political sentiment had swung away from him. North Carolina declined at first to ratify the Federal Constitution, which he favored, and he himself failed of election to the state convention. He died in 1790 at the age of forty-eight. By his marriage to Anne Clark of Wilmington he had two sons and a daughter.

Arthur Middleton

Thos Heyward Junr.

Edward Rutledge /.

Thomas Lynch Junr.

227

The South Carolinians comprised the youngest of all the groups of Signers, their average age being less than thirty. All of them belonged to the plantation aristocracy, and the aggregate wealth of the families they represented made them one of the richest delegations. All four of them received training in the law in England, at the Middle Temple, though their predominant interest was in the agriculture which supported them so lavishly. Colonial South Carolinians of the topmost economic and social class were very often educated abroad and entrusted with important public duties at an early age. In this instance, however, the relative immaturity of the group was partly owing to the fact that so many mature leaders were occupied with public affairs in the province itself in the spring of 1776, when a constitution was adopted and a provincial government set up. Unlike the Virginians, however, the South Carolinians did not yet think they were separating from the mother country, and until July 2 the attitude of their delegates in Congress on the issue of independence was uncertain. They finally joined with the other delegations for purposes of unanimity, and this was a conspicuous instance of co-operation. But even at this stage they were notable for their passionate devotion to their own locality and not one of their representatives looked like a real revolutionist. What they most wanted then and for generations thereafter was local independence.

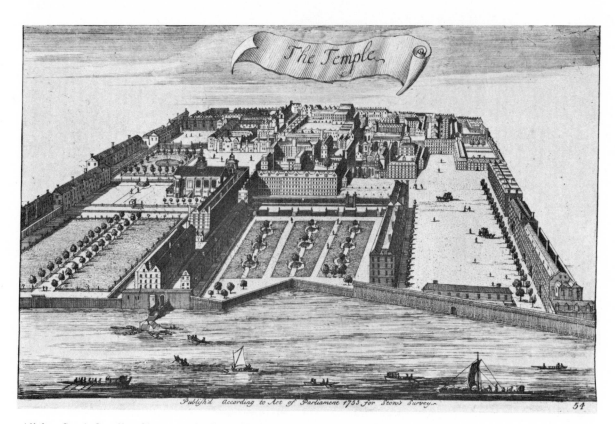

All four South Carolina Signers received training in law at the Middle Temple, London.

Arthur Middleton and his wife and son were painted during a visit to England.

ARTHUR MIDDLETON at thirty-four was the oldest Signer from South Carolina and he came from what was probably the richest family. Born at 'Middleton Place' on the Ashley River near Charleston, whose gardens are so famous in our own times, he was the son of Henry Middleton, who owned a score of plantations and some 800 slaves. Arthur, the eldest son of the house, was largely educated in England. He became and remained an excellent Latin and Greek scholar, afterward reading Horace and other classical writers for relief from public affairs. Also, he read law at the Middle Temple. The charming painting of him and his wife and infant son was made by Benjamin West on the occasion of a visit to England in his late twenties.

He was of middle size, well-formed, with great muscular strength and fine features, and he is reputed to have had a violent temper. A cultivated and capricious aristocrat, he was at the same time public-spirited.

A member of the provincial Assembly in his mid-twenties, he was again in that body in his early thirties; and as the controversy with the mother country reached its climax in 1774–76 he came to be regarded as a leader of the extreme Patriots. Despite his English education, he was ruthless toward Loyalists. Like other leaders in South Carolina, he was motivated chiefly by local patriotism and was no sort of economic or social radical. He was a member of the council of safety which virtually ruled the province until a provisional government was set up in the spring of 1776, and he was a member of the large committee that drew the constitution for the latter.

His activity in these provincial affairs delayed his departure for Congress. There in effect he succeeded his father, who had once been president of that body but took a more moderate position than he in the imperial controversy. It was after May 1776 that Arthur Middleton took his seat. He was re-elected the next year but never spent much time in the sessions in Philadelphia. He spoke frequently when present but did not like routine business. The story is that he refused to serve on the committee on accounts, saying that he hated accounts and did not even keep

Middleton Place, the remaining wing of which is shown here, was his home in Charleston.

230

He was buried at Middleton Place.

his own. As an officer of the militia, he was imprisoned by the British after the fall of Charleston, along with his fellow-Signers Heyward and Rutledge, and confined for some months at St. Augustine.

He died in 1787 in his forty-fifth year and was buried at 'Middleton Place.' His wife, Mary Izard, bore him nine children. His son Henry, the infant in Benjamin West's painting, did much to embellish 'Middleton Place,' planting the first camellias there, though the azaleas were not started until the next generation. Another son, John Izard Middleton, who became noted in his time as an archaeologist, spent most of his life abroad. Arthur Middleton's daughter married Daniel Elliott Huger, later a judge, and the connections of the Signer comprise practically a social register of eighteenth-century South Carolina. Edward Rutledge and Charles Cotesworth Pinckney were his brothers-in-law.

Thomas Heyward, Jr., Arthur Middleton, and Edward Rutledge, captured by the British, were imprisoned at St. Augustine.

231

THOMAS HEYWARD, Jr., who turned thirty in the month that the Declaration of Independence was adopted, was next to the oldest of the Signers from South Carolina and, like all the rest of them, was a member of the landed aristocracy. Born on his father's plantation in St. Helena's (later St. Luke's) Parish, he read law at the Middle Temple and began practice in the province at the age of twenty-five. He was in England during the earlier stages of the imperial controversy but was projected into public life almost immediately after his return and was an active Patriot from the time of the Coercive Acts against Boston. His local career closely paralleled that of Arthur Middleton, and he did not go to the Continental Congress until after a provisional government had been set up in South Carolina in the spring of 1776. The precise position which he took before July 2 on the still-unsettled question of independence is uncertain, but Dr. Benjamin Rush described him as a 'firm republican,' saying at the same time that he was a man of good education and most amiable manners who had 'an elegant poetical genius.' He was literary as congressmen went, but the fruits of his genius were not widely displayed to public view.

Heyward remained in Congress through 1778, then returning to his home state to become a circuit judge. As an artillery officer he participated in fighting on several occasions during the war, and he was captured when Charleston fell, being afterward imprisoned at

Susanna Savage Heyward.

St. Augustine with Middleton and Rutledge. Following the war he rendered legislative and judicial service in the state, but at the age of forty-three he retired to devote himself to his plantation. He was the first president of the Agricultural Society of South Carolina. Like other wealthy planters, he maintained a fine town house in Charleston, and this was occupied by President Washington on a visit to that lovely city in his first administration.

Heyward lived longest of the Signers from South Carolina, dying in 1809 in his sixty-third year. He was twice married—to Elizabeth Mathewes and to Susanna Savage—and had many descendants by both marriages.

Heyward's home, Charleston.

233

EDWARD RUTLEDGE, who at the age of twenty-six and a half was the youngest of the Signers of the Declaration, was also by force of circumstances and his own personality the most articulate member of the South Carolina delegation during the most crucial weeks of the struggle over independence. A younger brother of John Rutledge, he was born in Charlestown (Charleston) and read law in the Middle Temple, returning home from England early in 1773, when he was twenty-three. About a year later he married Henrietta Middleton, sister of Arthur.

Members of the plantation aristocracy entered prominently into public life at an amazingly early age, and young Rutledge was a member of the first Continental Congress before he was twenty-five. There he excited the scorn of John Adams, never an admirer of the South Carolinians, who thus described him: 'Young Ned Rutledge is a perfect Bob-o-Lincoln—a swallow, a sparrow, a peacock; excessively vain, excessively weak, and excessively variable and unsteady; jejeune, inane, and puerile.' At first young Ned may have seemed the capricious echo of his brother John, who long held hopes of reconciliation with the mother country, but he was re-elected to the second Congress, and in the spring of 1776 he was actually the most experienced member of the depleted delegation from his province. His brother John had returned home, where he became the first president under the provisional government, and other more mature leaders, like the elder Middleton, had also gone back. Young Rutledge is generally held responsible for the postponement of the vote on the resolution of independence, and his attitude was the natural result of his uncertainty about the sentiment of South Carolina. He is also given the major credit for the decision of the delegation to go along with the others on July 2 for the sake of unanimity, though Arthur Middleton and Heyward had arrived before that time and it is hard to know just what went on behind the scenes.

Rutledge returned to the Low Country in the autumn of 1776, served as an officer in the militia and as a representative in the state legislature, and, though re-elected to Congress a little later, he did not get back to Philadelphia. Along with Middleton and Heyward, he was captured when Charleston fell and was imprisoned in St. Augustine. After the war he was ac-

Rutledge's home, Charleston.

EDWARD RUTLEDGE

tive in the legislature and in state conventions. In no sense democratic in his ideas, he was a staunch Federalist in national politics, but as a presidential elector in 1796 he voted for Pinckney and Jefferson, not Pinckney and John Adams. The other electors from his state did likewise, but, whether consciously or not, he had avenged himself on the New Englander who once had scorned him. The jejeune statesman put on weight and lost most of his hair as he grew older. In his home country he had always been thought a genial and charming gentleman, and no doubt he mellowed with the years. In 1798 he became governor of his state, but he died in 1800 before completing his term. He was only a few months past fifty. His first wife, Henrietta Middleton, bore him three children, but his second marriage, to Mrs. Mary Shubrick Eveleigh, was childless. He was buried in St. Philip's Churchyard, Charleston, where lie the remains of John C. Calhoun and other famous South Carolinians.

THOMAS LYNCH, Jr., who was twenty-seven in the summer of 1776 and only a few months older than Edward Rutledge, was elected as a delegate to Congress to care for, and if necessary to substitute for, his father, Thomas Lynch, Sr.—who had a stroke early in the year and was virtually incapacitated until his death toward the end of 1776. The father was the grandson of an Irishman who had established the family fortunes as a rice planter in the Low Country and was himself a prosperous and highly respected man. He was rather more radical on the imperial question than most of the planters of South Carolina were—possibly because of his Irish tradition. He had given his son an English education, nonetheless.

The younger Lynch, who became a Signer somewhat by accident, was born in Prince George's Parish, South Carolina; and after attending Eton and Cambridge he read law in the Middle Temple. He did not long practice law, which he disliked, but became a planter and, through his father's influence, was elected to

local public office at an early age. He never re-
covered from a spell of bilious fever, and from
1775 onward his health was precarious. For this
reason he remained in Congress only a short
time after signing the Declaration. His father
died on the way home and his own health grew
worse under these trying circumstances. Several years earlier he had married Elizabeth
Shubrick. In the year 1779, when he was thirty,
he and she embarked for the West Indies, expecting to sail from there to southern France.
They were never heard of thereafter and were
presumed to have been lost at sea. No other
Signer had so short a life or so sad a story.

Mrs. Lynch.

Lynch's birthplace, Hopsewee, Santee, South Carolina.

237

238

Lyman Hall *Button Gwinnett*

Geo Walton.

The colony of Georgia was much the youngest of the thirteen, and at the outbreak of the American Revolution its settled area comprised little more than a strip along the coast and up the Savannah River. Much the larger part of the present state was then occupied by Indians. It is not surprising that Loyalist sentiment was strong in what was virtually a British frontier outpost, and that all of the Signers from Georgia were born outside of the province. One of them was a physician and a planter, another a planter who had been a merchant, and a third a young lawyer who had made his own way. They were no such aristocrats as the South Carolinians but were more consistently favorable to independence.

LYMAN HALL, at fifty-two the oldest of the Signers from Georgia, was the earliest leader among the Patriots in that remote and sparsely settled province. Born at Wallingford, Connecticut, he was a graduate of Yale, and after spending some not wholly successful years as a minister he became a physician. In 1775 he was living in a settlement of New Englanders and persons of New England descent in St. John's Parish on the Georgia coast below Savannah. This was called Sunbury and he had helped establish it seventeen or eighteen years earlier. Here as a physician and rice planter, Hall, who was a large and likeable man, became a leading figure. He had brought with him the spirit of political independence which he had imbibed in Connecticut, so long a self-governing colony, and Sunbury became a focal center of the Patriot cause in a relatively indifferent region where Loyalism was strong.

Hall was elected a delegate to the Continental Congress by his parish in the spring of 1775 and was admitted to the intercolonial body,

though denied a vote. At the meeting of a Georgia provincial congress in the summer he was regularly elected, and he was re-elected in 1776, when Button Gwinnett and George Walton were chosen for the first time. When he and Gwinnett arrived on May 20, John Adams described them as 'intelligent and spirited men, who made a powerful addition to our phalanx.' Walton arrived a little later. Because of the 'remote situation' of Georgia, the provincial congress had avoided giving specific instructions. The delegates were left free to exercise their best judgment but in the Continental Congress there never was any doubt where they stood.

Hall remained a member of that body until 1780, bringing his family north when the British destroyed his home and plantation in 1778. After the war he moved to Savannah to practice medicine, and in 1783 he became governor of Georgia. During his brief term he recommended the setting aside of a grant of land for the support of a college. From this beginning came Franklin College and the University of Georgia, the first state institution of the sort to be chartered. Actually, it did not open until some years later, after Lyman Hall was dead, but it owed its actual start to another son of Connecticut and graduate of Yale, Abraham Baldwin. These transplanted New Englanders served well their adopted state.

Hall was twice married—to Abigail Burr and to Mary Osborn, both of Fairfield, Connecticut —and he had a son by his second marriage. He died in 1790, at the age of sixty-six, on the plantation in Burke County to which he had retired. He was buried there but his remains were removed half a century later to Augusta, where a monument was erected to him and George Walton.

An obelisk in Augusta commemorates Lyman Hall and George Walton, who are buried there.

BUTTON GWINNETT, who was forty-one in 1776, was born in England at Down Hatherley, Gloucestershire, and was of Welsh ancestry on the side of his father, a clergyman. At the age of thirty he and his English wife, Ann Bourne of Wolverhampton, were in Savannah, where for a time he was a merchant. Then he bought St. Catherine's Island off the coast and became a planter. During the decade before the Revolution he was occupied chiefly with his own involved affairs, but he was drawn into public activities by Lyman Hall, who lived not far away at Sunbury on the mainland. He shared the patriotic sentiments of Hall and the settlers of New England stock in that district. He had already been a member of the provincial Assembly, but his prominence dates from his election in 1776 as a delegate to the Continental Congress. He arrived in Philadelphia with Hall in May, duly voted for and signed the Declaration, and returned to Georgia late in the summer.

He is said to have been a big, well-proportioned, and mannerly person, and also to have been high-tempered. He is supposed to have been the chief draftsman of the first Georgia constitution, adopted by the provisional Assembly in February 1777. This constitution was similar to that of Pennsylvania in that it had a unicameral legislature that completely dominated the government, and the claim was afterward made that Gwinnett had brought a copy of the Pennsylvania constitution back with him from Philadelphia. Whether he did or did not, both of these early frames of government had to be modified and strengthened within a dozen years or so.

Gwinnett's public ambitions at this stage appear to have been military, but, following the death of Archibald Bulloch, he became for a couple of months the chief executive of the young state and was drawn into a controversy with the military authorities, especially Brigadier General Lachlan McIntosh. This became acute when an investigation of an unsuccessful expedition into Florida resulted in the vindication of the civil authority. When McIntosh called Gwinnett a scoundrel and liar, a duel ensued in which both men were wounded. This occurred outside Savannah, and Gwinnett died

a few days later, on May 16, 1777, at the age of forty-two. Presumably, he was buried in Savannah.

He left little except debts, and his rare autographs are supposed to be more valuable than those of any other Signer. On the engrossed parchment his name appears farthest to the left, first among the Georgians; and thus, reading from left to right, his signature comes first after that of President John Hancock. Yet of all the Signers he lacked only one of being the first to die.

Gwinnett lived in this tree-shaded house on St. Catherine's Island off the coast.

243

GEORGE WALTON, aged thirty-five, was mistakenly supposed by some of his contemporaries to have been the youngest Signer—perhaps because of his small size. Born near Farmville, Virginia, he was orphaned early, apprenticed to a carpenter, and largely self-taught. He moved to Savannah in his late twenties and in 1776 was a practicing lawyer there. From the time of the Boston Tea Party he had been an active Patriot, serving on the council of safety and as secretary of the provincial congress in 1775. Elected to the Continental Congress in 1776, he arrived in Philadelphia a little after Hall and Gwinnett, and he is said to have been somewhat less 'radical' than they, but he stood with them unquestionably for political independence.

He was in Congress when the Georgia state constitution was adopted, but he took the side of Lachlan McIntosh in the controversy which continued after Button Gwinnett fell in their duel. He was a colonel of militia in the siege of Savannah in 1778, and was wounded, captured, and exchanged; and he was several weeks governor of the state before the British and Loyalists largely took it over. During most of the period from 1776 to the end of the fighting, however, he was in Congress, serving on important committees and making himself a useful member. With his fellow Signer, George Taylor, he negotiated a treaty with the Iroquois, and after leaving Congress he negotiated one with the Cherokee Indians.

In Georgia he was chief justice during the Confederation period and he held other judicial posts later, being a notable supporter of law and order in his rather turbulent state, then in a frontier stage. In 1789 he became governor and in the last decade of his life he filled an unexpired term in the United States Senate. He appears to have grown more conservative with advancing years, and he was identified with the Federalists in national politics. He played a constuctive part in the early history of the University of Georgia. During his last years he lived in Augusta, which became the capital during his administration as governor. Though violent in temper and sometimes imperious in manner, he was greatly respected. He married Dorothy Camber and had two sons. He died in 1804 at the age of sixty-three in Augusta, and his remains now lie with those of Lyman Hall beneath a monument erected there in the middle of the nineteenth century.

Meadow Garden, Walton's home, Augusta.

245

PART *Three*

THE DECLARATION
UNTIL NOW

The Fortunes

of

A SACRED DOCUMENT

IT is doubtful if, at the outset, many people regarded the Declaration as a sacred document. In 1776 the *act* of declaring independence was the matter of paramount importance, and the supreme task of the Patriots throughout the war was to achieve the freedom which they had claimed. Indeed, this task was not completed, this goal was not fully attained, until after another war. Not until after 1815, when treaties of peace closed the War of 1812 and brought to an end two decades of fierce conflict in Europe, could it be truly said that American independence had been completed. Then, in the flush of national patriotism and self-consciousness, attention was focused, as it had not been previously, on the symbol of independence which had often been in hiding and generally in obscurity.

The value of this symbol has been enhanced with the passing years, but not until our own generation, when the Nation has gained stature such as the Fathers did not dream of, has the first and greatest charter of the American Republic been fully enshrined as a *document*. The place it has held in the hearts of the people cannot be measured in terms of the physical care or neglect of it, to be sure, but there is significance as well as interest in its physical history.

BACK of the STATE HOUSE, PHILADELPHIA

EARLY TRAVELS OF A ROLL OF PARCHMENT

AT THE BEGINNING, the Declaration was just another congressional paper in the keeping of Secretary Charles Thomson. From the time that it was engrossed on parchment and signed, it assumed a different physical character and it may have been guarded with more than average care; but, in a period when the government had no permanent seat and actually consisted of nothing but the Continental Congress, it had to follow the peregrinations of that wandering legislature.

Toward the end of 1776, Congress, alarmed by the near approach of the enemy to Philadelphia, adjourned to Baltimore. The records and papers of that body, including the Declaration, were removed by wagon to the Maryland city, and it was there that the document was printed for a second time and given forth for the first time with the names of the various Signers. In the spring of 1777 Congress returned to Philadelphia, but the first anniversary of the Declaration appears to have passed unnoticed, and in the autumn the governing body of the struggling young Republic again fled. This time Congress went to Lancaster and then to York, Pennsylvania, where the Declaration was stored in the courthouse. It was back in Philadelphia before its second birthday, and the annual celebrations which have ever since continued seem to date from July 4, 1778.

Courthouse, York, Pennsylvania.

A Front View of the State-House &c. at ANNAPOLIS the Capital of MARYLAND.

Broad Street, Wall Street, and New York City Hall in 1797.

For about five years, until July 1783, the roll of parchment remained in the State House in Philadelphia where it had originally been signed, then it started on another series of journeys—as Congress moved to Princeton, Trenton, Annapolis, and in June 1785, to New York. There it was stored in the City Hall on Wall Street, in which, remodeled as Federal Hall according to plans of L'Enfant, George Washington was inaugurated in 1789. The Secretary of Congress delivered the Declaration to President Washington, and it was in custody of the Secretary of State from the time there was such an official.

Until the spring of 1790, John Jay, who had handled foreign affairs for the Confederation, was acting Secretary, besides being Chief Justice, but after a time Thomas Jefferson arrived from France by way of Monticello and took charge of the new office and the document he had drafted. It may be assumed that he kept it in his temporary offices on lower Broadway, and that it was removed to his departmental quarters on Market Street, Philadelphia, when, in 1790, the government began its ten-year stay in that city. The Declaration had returned to its birthplace and for three years was in the custody of its author, until he returned to Monticello early in 1794. Until 1800, the roll of parchment remained in Philadelphia in the charge of successive secretaries of state, who probably did not unroll it often if they ever did. By this time Jefferson, at least, was aware of its historic importance. In a reminiscent moment in the year 1800, he drew in private a list of achievements of his which he deemed memorable and this included the authorship of the Declaration.

When the Government moved to Washington, pictured here with adjacent Georgetown a few months later, the Declaration came with it.

A PERILOUS QUARTER-CENTURY

THE NEW FEDERAL CITY OF WASHINGTON, arising beside the Potomac at a place of George Washington's choosing, was a city only in name when the government moved there, bag and baggage, in the autumn of 1800. To all save prophets and dreamers it looked like a wilderness of trees and a sea of mud. John Adams, uncomfortably settled with his wife, Abigail, in the unfinished Executive Mansion, was in his last months as President, and lanky John Marshall, soon to be Chief Justice, was Secretary of State. Jefferson took over the presidential office in the following March and this rural philosopher found the rural capital more endurable than his predecessor had.

Unquestionably he was conscious of the significance of the Declaration as a document and he and his Secretary of State, James Madison, were not likely to be careless with it, but they had to avail themselves of such storage facilities as there were. During most of the time until 1814 it was in the War Office Building on Seventeenth Street.

In the summer of that year it was removed under exceedingly perilous circumstances. Madison was then President and this was the last year of the War of 1812. The invasion of the Chesapeake Bay region by the British was without military significance, but the devastation they wrought by fire in Washington and the flight of the government before them marked a low point in national humiliation. Before they got to the capital the Secretary of State, James Monroe, fortunately had the papers of his department, including the Declaration, packed in linen sacks and taken elsewhere. The sacred document remained for a night in a barn a couple of miles from Chain Bridge, and then it was stored in the house of a clergyman named Littlejohn in Leesburg, Virginia. Meanwhile, Dolly Madison, before escaping from the Executive Mansion, had the Stuart portrait of George Washington taken from its frame and carried to a place of safety.

Fortunately, the British did not linger long; and the Executive Mansion, which had been blackened with smoke, soon appeared in a glistening garb of white paint which made it worthy of its historic name. The war turned out better in the end than anybody had reason to expect, and the country and its sacred relics were never again to be exposed to danger at British hands. The Declaration was brought back from the clergyman's house in Leesburg, and a few years later (1820), when the Department of State had begun to occupy a building on the site of the present Treasury, the document was stored there.

It had ceased, however, to languish in obscurity. Until the time of the War of 1812 it had appeared only in print, but the patriotic public was soon given the chance to see how it looked in writing. In 1816 John Binns, publisher of the *Democratic Press* in Philadelphia and an Irishman by birth, announced his intention of issuing an engraved copy of the charter with signatures, but a professional penman, Benjamin Owen Tyler, got ahead of him.

When the British raided Washington the Declaration was moved again.

253

The fire-blackened President's House was painted white.

The Declaration was lodged in this Department of State building.

Tyler copied the Declaration and imitated the signatures so well that Richard Rush, the Secretary of State and the son of a Signer, thought them practically undistinguishable from the originals. This engraving was published in 1818, when national patriotism was surging. John Binns, attacking his rival in print, got his own engraving on the market the next year. In this, the text and signatures were surrounded by the seals of the states, while pictures of Washington, John Hancock, and Jefferson adorned the top. This was taking some liberties, since the famous General had been about his military duties in 1776 and was not a Signer of the Declaration, but apparently the public did not mind. Both of these engravings were private commercial ventures and did well.

A few years later (1823) the Secretary of State, John Quincy Adams, son of one of the important Signers, had an exact facsimile made, unadorned by seals and portraits. It was the only real facsimile and has been the basis of all later ones. Two copies were sent to each of the few surviving Signers, Jefferson's being on parchment; copies were given high officials and still others were distributed throughout the country. Thus did the Declaration, as it actually looked, become a familiar sight a half a century after it was engrossed on parchment.

One result of this renewed interest in the charter of 1776, during the period of highly vocal patriotism following the War of 1812, was a controversy about the authorship of the paper. This was started with a speech on July 4, 1823, by Timothy Pickering, who had been one of the bitterest of the High Federalists; and its main design was to minimize Jefferson's part in the work of composition and to reflect unfavorably on him in general. Jefferson, who was eighty and living in deserved quiet at Monticello, entered into no newspaper controversy, but in private he penned recollections which have been of great value to modern-day students trying to reconstruct the story of events in 1776. Also, in a later private letter he disavowed all claim of originality on his own part. It was then that he said that his main object had been 'to place before mankind the common sense of the subject,' and that the Declaration was intended to be 'an expression of the American mind.' The greatness of his pride in the most famous work of his hand was unmistakably revealed by his instructions for his tombstone, but he regarded the Declaration as no personal creation; it was an American charter which should be above and beyond partisanship, and he hoped that its principles would be recognized as eternal. The partisan controversy which was initiated and continued by ancient foes may have clouded the air for a time, but it served posterity by shedding light on the circumstances and meaning of the Declaration. It created no lasting breach between him and Adams, who breathed his name on the day they both lay dying.

In purely physical terms, the results of the renewed interest in the historic document were bad. While immortal in spirit it was by no means imperishable in form. Secretary Richard Rush perceived the hand of time upon it when Benjamin Owen Tyler copied it; and many experts have believed that the processes employed in making the official facsimile tended to loosen the ink. Apparently the parchment was always

Tyler issued the first reproduction of the engrossed Declaration. The first three men to sign the subscription book were Jefferson, Madison, and J. Q. Adams.

rolled and never folded, but the effects of frequent unrolling and rerolling could not fail to be deleterious. Least injury was done the text and greatest was done the signatures, which had been written at various times in various qualities of ink and were most rubbed in the process of rolling, since they were at the bottom.

John Binns marketed this ornamental engraving of the Declaration.

EXPOSURE AND OBSCURITY

BEGINNING in 1820, the document was kept in the building occupied by the Department of State, where it appears to have been little disturbed after the facsimile was made. Its health was not improved when, in 1841, Secretary of State Webster ordered it placed in the new Patent Office building. No doubt this was a safer repository than the earlier ones, but during the generation that the Declaration remained there it hung on the wall in a frame, along with George Washington's commission as Commander in Chief. Opposite a window, it was exposed to the 'chill of winter and the glare and heat of summer.' Fading was inevitable under such circumstances, and the yellowing of the parchment was noted by observers. When it was exhibited at the Centennial celebration in Philadelphia in 1876, the text was still legible but many of the signatures were so dim as to be virtually unrecognizable and some had become invisible.

At the age of one hundred years the document had become truly venerable. It was read in Philadelphia on July 4 by a grandson of Richard Henry Lee, the man who had pre-sented the resolutions leading to it, and at the sight of it the crowd burst into cheers. During the Exposition it was kept in a fireproof safe, behind a plate glass door. Then, despite the efforts of the Philadelphians to keep it in the city of its birth, it was brought back to Washington in 1877 and exhibited for seventeen more years in the Department of State.

Meanwhile, there had been anxious official inquiry into its physical state. A proposal by a skilled penman to retrace the writing came to naught, and happily no effort was made to restore it by chemicals. But the necessity of protecting the document from light was imperative, and at length, in 1894, exhibition of it ceased except on rare occasions and on direct order of the Secretary of State. It was then 118 years old. Sealed between two plates of glass and locked in a safe, it remained in dark obscurity for more than a quarter of a century, while William Jennings Bryan was orating about Free Silver and Theodore Roosevelt was brandishing the Big Stick, and American doughboys were fighting in the First World War.

Moved to the Patent Office, the Declaration faded as it hung on a wall.

*Flags flew and Independence Hall was the focal point
of the Centennial anniversary observance of the Signing.*

INDEPENDENCE HALL *became a shrine.*

259

The Fourth today: fireworks over Washington Monument.

Young America celebrates the Fourth: 1867.

Fourth of July: 1859.

THE DAY WE CELEBRATE

260

Fireworks in the country: 1869.

Picnicking on the Fourth: 1864.

*Richard Henry Lee, a descendant of the Signer, read
the Declaration as a part of the 1876 celebration.*

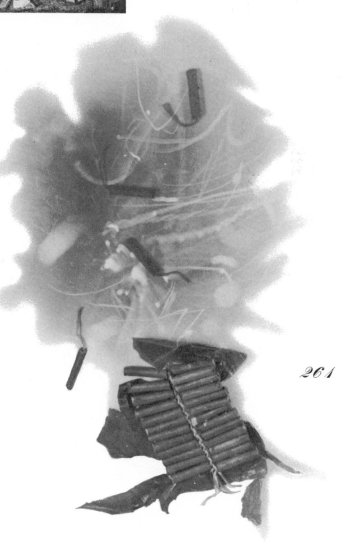

261

THE LAST GENERATION

IT WAS IN THE NINETEEN-TWENTIES, after the storm of war had subsided, that the Declaration was brought from its hiding place into a world that seemed to offer it both security and visibility. That the physical body of the great charter of liberty must be preserved was recognized, but men were asking if there was sufficient reason for it to be wholly veiled from sight. In the generation of interment it had occasionally been examined and photographed; and not long after the First World War it was viewed afresh by a committee of experts. They concluded that it ought to be consigned to the most competent of custodians, but that it might be exhibited under careful safeguards. Specifically, it should be hermetically sealed between sheets of glass and exposed only to diffused light. It could not withstand the broad glare of day but it could survive the dim light of an archival sanctuary.

A few months later the Secretary of State, Charles E. Hughes, recommended that it be transferred to the Library of Congress, where it would unquestionably receive expert care and might be safely exhibited to the curious and admiring public. President Harding issued the appropriate order and on September 30, 1921, the document, then 145 years old, was trans-ported with unpretentious care to Capitol Hill. There for a time it remained in the office of Dr. Herbert Putnam, Librarian of Congress. That other supremely sacred document, the Constitution of the United States, had also been transferred to the Library; and within a few months Congress made appropriations for what came to be called a shrine. This was designed by Francis H. Bacon, whose brother planned the Lincoln Memorial, and it was erected on the second floor of the Library under the direction of David Lynn, Architect of the Capitol.

On February 29, 1924, there was a simple ceremony of dedication, attended by President and Mrs. Coolidge, Secretary Hughes, and a representative group from Congress. Dr. Putnam enshrined the Declaration and the Constitution by the simple process of putting them in their places, and the spectators then sang 'America.' Here the sacred relics remained until the attack on Pearl Harbor again involved the United States in world war and, for safety's sake, they were placed in hiding. They were stored with the gold at Fort Knox, Kentucky, in the heart of the North American continent. There was a grim symbolism in these events, for war is no more a respecter of cherished

A Library of Congress truck takes the Declaration to its new home: 1921.

President and Mrs. Coolidge attend the dedication of the shrine at the Library of Congress.

symbols than it is of persons, and the wide oceans had ceased to provide adequate protection.

On the day after Christmas in 1941, the Declaration and the Constitution were removed from the shrine, packed with the utmost care in a bronze container of special design, and taken to the Union Station. Thence they were borne in a Pullman compartment to Kentucky, in the care of the Chief Assistant Librarian and under the guard of Secret Service men. As it were, the Crown jewels of the Nation were being carried to an underground treasure house. Next day the documents were deposited in a vault at Fort Knox, and there they remained until the autumn of 1944. During this period of more than two and a half years the older and more damaged of them, the Declaration, was inspected several times, under proper atmospheric conditions, by experts. After it had been unmounted, glue and other adherent ma-

terial were removed from it, cracks were drawn together, and it was otherwise repaired.

On October 1, 1944, the Declaration and the Constitution were again displayed to public view in the shrine at the Library of Congress, with a Marine guard beside it, who was relieved by Army and Navy guards in rotation. Freedom and representative government, if not yet fully triumphant, seemed reasonably secure in a war-torn world. Speaking of the 'sheets of vellum and leaves of ancient paper' which were thus re-enshrined and protected the Librarian of Congress, Archibald Mac-Leish, said: 'Nothing that men have ever made surpasses them.'

In these later years of national maturity and self-consciousness, accompanied by scientific knowledge which would have dumbfounded the Fathers of the Republic, no care has been too great to lavish on these sacred documents. The Bureau of Standards made a close study of the problem of preserving them, further protective measures being taken on its recommendation and with the co-operation of its technicians. The documents were sealed in insulating glass; the air was expelled and special

The Declaration remained at the Library until the Japanese attack on Pearl Harbor.

263

paper of cellulose was put behind the Declaration in order to absorb moisture and offset changes in temperature; a new lighting system was installed. Presumably, science could do more to render this old bit of parchment imperishable, and we can be sure that if further discoveries should be made and further safeguards be suggested, the present custodians of the Declaration will fully avail themselves of them.

Not unnaturally it had been supposed that the shrine in the Library of Congress, where, among others, a future Queen of England and future Pope viewed the great charter, would be a permanent repository as well as a safe one. But that was before the National Archives building. The purpose of this new building was to store the official records of the government—as against books and newspapers and more personal papers—and one of its halls was specially designed to house and exhibit the most famous of the Nation's documents. Thus the transfer of the Declaration to another home and shrine was necessitated by the law of the land. The departure of the sacred relic from the Library of Congress was more solemn and ceremonial than its original arrival had been—when it was brought in a mail truck and deposited in a safe in the Librarian's office. On December 13, 1952, in company with the Constitution, it was borne down the steps by guards from all the armed services, transported in a tank which breathed defiance against all foreign and domestic enemies, and escorted by service men and women to the National Archives building. There on December 15, it was

again displayed to the public, along with the somewhat less venerable Constitution and Bill of Rights. The ceremonies accompanying this event were more elaborate than earlier ones in the Library of Congress. The various states were officially represented and state flags were much in evidence. The Chief Justice presided; the Chairman of the Joint Congressional Committee on the Library unveiled the shrine; and the President of the United States delivered an address.

The older the Declaration has grown, the more formal and ceremonial we have become about it, and its present shrine may be regarded as a sarcophagus within which it lies embalmed. But those timeworn phrases and dim autographs can come alive in the minds of the men and women and children who gaze upon it in reverent curiosity. As the author of this precious document once said, 'the earth belongs always to the living generation,' and it is only in the human heart, at last, that the Declaration can be vested with immortality.

In 1951 the Declaration was given a new case at the Bureau of Standards.

Ceremony marked the departure of the Declaration and Constitution from the Library of Congress in December 1952.

The Declaration was well shielded during the trip of a few blocks to the National Archives.

At the National Archives the Declaration comes to rest again.

What It Means Now

UNLIKE the Constitution, the Declaration of Independence provides no frame of government. It offers no pattern for human society, no specific program for the present, no blueprint for the future. But, unless its author was very much mistaken, it contains a body of abiding truth. The apotheosis of the Constitution in our own land may be regarded as symbolic of our devotion to a government of laws, not men. But the enshrined Declaration is a perpetual reminder of the purpose of these laws, of the only valid purpose of all laws—to provide a society within which *all* men can enjoy the largest feasible degree of liberty and attain the fullest measure of happiness.

If hearts are still stirred by the Declaration, as they surely are, this is partly because of its historic associations, partly because of the beauty of its phrases, but chiefly because men perceive within it the quality of universality. The historic American faith, which Congress made official on July 4, 1776, can be simply stated in dateless language:

By birth all men are equal, not in ability or condition, for that has been untrue in all the ages of which we have any record, but in the possession of fundamental rights. Life, liberty, and the pursuit of happiness are mentioned in the great Charter; but more important than any list is the 'truth' that men possess these rights, not because of race or creed or station, but because they are human beings. Here is the eternal answer to bigotry and intolerance of any and every sort.

Thousands visit the shrine each year and see the living Declaration.

Government and every other form of public control is a means to human well-being, not an end in itself. Man is not made for the state but the state for man, and it derives its just *powers only from the consent of the governed. In extreme cases, like the one in 1776, this 'truth' justifies political revolution, and in all cases it provides the criterion by which any government or institution should be judged. No sort of rule can justly rest on power alone, and here is the eternal answer to all forms of tyranny over the persons, the property, and the minds of men.*

The wondrous phrases which were written on our first Independence Day into the official creed of the newborn Republic were an expression of ideals, not a description of immediate realities. In every generation since that time some men have scoffed at them, others have done only lip-service to them, and still others have been distressed by the slow and imperfect attainment of them. But the gradual realization of the implications of the great Declaration constitutes the history of American democracy; and, outside of the sacred religious writings, this document more than any other has inspired our citizens and statesmen to their noblest actions.

It has never received more eloquent testimony than that of Abraham Lincoln. There was poignant drama in his brief visit to Philadelphia, on his way to Washington to be inaugurated as President. On Washington's birthday in 1861, speaking in Independence Hall, he said:

...I have never had a feeling politically that did not spring from the sentiments embodied in the Declaration of Independence....I have often inquired of myself what great principle or idea it was that kept this Confederacy so long together. It was not the mere matter of the separation of the Colonies from the motherland; but that sentiment in the Declaration of Independence which gave liberty, not alone to the people of this country, but, I hope, to the world, for all future time. It was that which gave promise that in due time the weight would be lifted from the shoulders of all men.

In our own century dictatorships and totalitarian governments have arisen that magnify the state at the expense of human freedom and dignity. Even in democratic societies like our own, the functions of government have been enormously enlarged in the effort to meet the vast international and domestic problems of our age. Meanwhile, the machines which have contributed so much to our prosperity, comfort, and convenience tend to overshadow and even threaten to overwhelm the individual. Times have greatly changed since 1776, but never more than today has there been such need to turn to our oldest and noblest charter for light and hope. The great Declaration still issues its ringing challenge to despotism in any guise, and it still proclaims the undying faith in human beings which has permeated and glorified the history of America.

A Selection of Colonial Broadsides, 1770-1775

To the Sons of Liberty in this City.

GENTLEMEN,

IT'S well known, that it has been the Custom of all Nations to erect Monuments to perpetuate the Remembrance of grand Events. Experience has proved, that they have had a good Effect on the Posterity of those who raised them, especially such as were made sacred to Liberty. Influenced by these Considerations, a Number of the Friends to Liberty in this City, erected a Pole in the Fields, on Ground belonging to the Corporation, as a temporary Memorial of the unanimous Opposition to the detestable Stamp-Act; which having been destroyed by some disaffected Persons, a Number of the Inhabitants determined to erect another, made several Applications to the Mayor, as the principal Member of the Corporation, for Leave to erect the new Pole in the Place where the old One stood. The Committee that waited on him the last Time, disposed to remove every Objection, apprehensive that some of the Corporation might be opposed to the Erection of the Pole, from a Supposition that those Citizens who were for its being raised, were actuated solely by a Party Spirit, offered when the Pole was finished to make it a Present to the Corporation, provided they would order it to be erected either where the other stood or near Mr. *Van De Bergh*'s, where the two Roads meet. But even this, astonishing as it may seem to Englishmen, was rejected by the Majority of the Corporation, and the other Requisitions denied. We question whether this Conduct can be paralleled by an Act of any Corporation in the British Dominions, chosen by the Suffrages of a free People.

And now, Gentlemen, seeing we are debarred the Privilege of public Ground to erect the Pole on, we have procured a Place for it near the Street between the House where *Katemut* used to live, and the Corner to the Westward, which is the most public Place that could be obtained. Your Attendance and Countenance are desired at Nine o'Clock on Tuesday Morning the 6th Instant, at Mr. *Crommelin*'s Wharf, in order to carry it up to be raised.

By Order of the Committee.

New-York, February 3, 1770.

Broadsides served a wide variety of purposes in an age when civil and cultural life were centered in a relatively few areas—the church, town hall, tavern, and market. Posted and passed around in those places, they informed the people of recently fought battles, deaths of the famous, murders and executions, of meetings to be held to discuss grievances. They were used to express private opinions and the prevailing sentiments of the times. They performed the present-day functions of "spot" news which radio and television provide.

BOSTON, DECEMBER 1, 1773.

GENTLEMEN,

THE Committee of Correspondence for this Town had just prepared their Letter covering the Proceedings of the Town at their two late Meetings of the 5th and 18th ultimo, when a Ship arrived from London with Part of the East-India Company's Teas : This induced us to forbear sending the Letters until we could procure some further Intelligence. On Monday last this and the neighbouring Towns as one Body convened at Faneuil-Hall, 'till the Assembly were so numerous as occasion'd an Adjournment to the Old South Meeting-House, where it was computed there was upwards of 5000 Persons, and then came into a Number of Votes and Resolves unanimously ; a Copy of which being handed to us by a Committee of that Body, we now forward to you, and are with great Esteem your Friends and humble Servants.

By Order of the Committee of Boston.

William Cooper Clerk

269

WE the Subscribers, inhabitants of the town of
having taken into our serious consideration the
precarious state of the liberties of North-America, and more
especially the present distressed condition of this insulted province,
embarrassed as it is by several acts of the British parliament, tending to
the entire subversion of our natural and charter rights ; among which is
the act for blocking up the harbour of Boston : and being fully sensible
of our indispensable duty to lay hold on every means in our power to
preserve and recover the much injured constitution of our country ; and
conscious at the same time of no alternative between the horrors of slavery,
or the carnage and desolation of a civil war, but a suspension of all commercial intercourse with the island of Great Britain, Do, in the presence
of God, solemnly and in good faith, covenant and engage with each
other, 1st, That from henceforth we will suspend all commercial intercourse with the said island of Great Britain, until the said act for blocking
up the said harbour be repealed, and a full restoration of our charter rights
be obtained.   And,

2ly, That there may be the less temptation to others to continue in
the said, now dangerous commerce, we do in like manner solemnly covenant that we will not buy, purchase or consume, or suffer any person,
by, for or under us to purchase or consume, in any manner whatever,
any goods, wares or merchandize which shall arrive in America from
Great Britain aforesaid, from and after the last day of August next ensuing.
And in order as much as in us lies to prevent our being interrupted and
defeated in this only peaceable measure, entered into for the recovery and
preservation of our rights, we agree to break off all trade, commerce
and dealings whatever with all persons, who, prefering their own private
interest to the salvation of their now perishing country, shall still continue
to import goods from Great Britain, or shall purchase of those who do
import, and never to renew any commerce or trade with them.

And, Whereas the promoting of industry, œconomy, arts and manufactures among ourselves is of the last importance to the civil and religious
welfare of a community ; we engage,

3ly, That from and after the first day of October next ensuing, we will,
not by ourselves, or any for, by, or under us, purchase or use any goods,
wares, manufactures or merchandize, whensoever or howsoever imported
from Great Britain, until the harbour of Boston shall be opened, and our
charter rights restored.   And,

Lastly, As a refusal to come into any agreement which promises the
deliverance of our country from the calamities it now feels, and which,
like a torrent are rushing upon it with increasing violence, must evidence
a disposition enimical to, or criminally negligent of, the common safety :
We agree, that after this covenant has been offered to any person, and
they refuse to sign it, we will consider them in the same light as contuma-
cious importers, and withdraw all commercial connexions with them
forever, and publish their names to the world. Witness our hands,
June,   1774.

270

ADVERTISEMENT.

THE Enemies of the Liberty of America, being unwearied in misrepresenting the Attachment of the Inhabitants of this City, to the common Cause of this Country, to the neighbouring Colonies, a Number of the Citizens think it highly necessary to conveen the good People of this Metropolis in the Fields on Wednesday next, which will be the 6th Instant, at Six o'Clock in the Evening; where every Friend to the true Interest of this distressed Country, is earnestly requested to attend---when Matters of the utmost Importance to their Reputation and Security, as Freemen, will be communicated.

TUESDAY, JULY 5th, 1774.

To the PUBLICK.

NEW-YORK, OCTOBER 5, 1774.

BY Mr. Rivere, who left Boston on Friday last, and arrived here last night, in his way to the General Congress, we have certain intelligence that the Carpenters and Masons who had inadvertently undertaken to erect barracks for the soldiers in that town, upon being informed that it was contrary to the sentiments of their countrymen, unanimously broke up, and returned to their respective homes, on the 26th of last month; which, it is hoped, will convince the Mechanicks of this city, how disagreeable it will be to the inhabitants of that place, for them to afford any manner of assistance to those, who are made subservient to the destruction of our American brethren.

Printed by JOHN HOLT, near the COFFEE-HOUSE.

271

In *Provincial Congress,*

Cambridge, *February* 14, 1775.

WHEREAS it appears necessary for the Defence of the Lives, Liberties, and Properties, of the Inhabitants of this Province, that this Congress on the first Day of their next Session, should be made fully acquainted with the Number and Military Equipments of the Militia, and Minute Men in this Province; and also the Town Stock of Ammunition in each Town and District :—

It is therefore RESOLVED, That it be and it is hereby recommended, to the commanding Officers of each Regiment of Minute Men, that now is or shall be formed in this Province, that they review the several Companies in their respective Regiments, or cause them to be reviewed, and take an exact State of their Numbers, and Equipment, —and where there is any Company that is not incorporated into a Regiment, the commanding Officer thereof shall review the several Companies, or cause them to be reviewed, and take a like State of their Numbers and Equipment—And it also recommended to the Colonels or commanding Officers of each Regiment of Militia in this Province, that they review the several Companies in their respective Regiments, or cause them to be reviewed, and take a State of their Numbers and Accoutrements ; which said State of the Minute Men and Militia, shall be by said Officers returned in Writing to this Congress, on the first Day of their Session after the Adjournment.———

And it is further RESOLVED, That it be recommended to the Select-Men of each Town and District in the Province, that on the same Day they make return in Writing of the State of the Town and District Stock of Ammunition, and War-like Stores to this Congress.

Signed by Order of the Provincial Congress,

JOHN HANCOCK, President.

A true Extract from the Minutes,

BENJAMIN LINCOLN, Secretary.

By the LION & UNICORN, Dieu & mon droit, *their Lieutenant-Generals, Governours, Vice Admirals, &c. &c. &c. &c.*

A HUE & CRY.

WHEREAS I have been informed, from undoubted authority, that a certain PATRICK HENRY, of the county of Hanover, and a number of *deluded followers,* have taken up arms, chosen their officers, and, ftyling themfelves an *independent company,* have marched out of their county, encamped, and put themfelves in a pofture of war; and have written and defpatched letters to divers parts of the country, exciting the people to join in thefe *outrageous* and *rebellious* practices, to the *great terrour* of all his Majefty's *faithful* fubjects, and in *open defiance* of *law* and *government* ; and have *committed other acts of violence,* particularly in *extorting* from his Majefty's *Receiver-General* the fum of 330l. under *pretence* of *replacing the powder* I *thought proper* to order from the magazine; whence it undeniably appears, there is *no longer* the leaft fecurity for the *life* or *property* of any man: Wherefore, I have *thought proper, with the advice of his Majefty's Council,* and *in his Majefty's name,* to iffue this *my* proclamation, ftrictly charging *all perfons,* upon their *allegiance,* not to *aid, abet,* or *give countenance* to the faid PATRICK HENRY, or *any other perfons* concerned in *fuch unwarrantable combinations;* but, on the contrary, to *oppofe them,* and *their defigns,* by *every means,* which defigns muft otherwife inevitably involve the *whole country* in the *moft direful calamity,* as they will call for the *vengeance* of *offended Majefty,* and the *infulted laws,* to be *exerted here,* to vindicate the *conftitutional* authority of government.

Given, &c. this 6th day of May, 1775.

D****.

G** d*** the P****.

Frefh ADVICES from the AMERICAN ARMY.

Camp at Cambridge, May 28, 1775.

YESTERDAY a Party from the United American Army was ordered to take the Cattle, Hay, &c. from Noddle's and Hog Iflands. While executing their Orders, they were attacked by a Number of the King's Troops from Bofton, in an armed Schooner, a Sloop, and 8 or 10 Boats belonging to the Men of War: A brifk Fire began about Four o'Clock, P. M. and continued moft of the Night, then ceafed a little, and at Dawn of Day was renewed, by which Time Capt. Fofter, with two Field Pieces from this Camp, joined our Troops, when a heavy Fire from the Shore on the armed Veffels put them into great Diftrefs. The Schooner's Decks were cleared, and fhe drifted on the Ferry-Way at Winefimet, where our People fat Fire to her, and fhe was foon blown up, and deftroyed. Sixteen Four-Pounders, and fix Swivels, were taken out of her by our People. The Sloop was difabled, and obliged to be towed off by the Men of War's Boats; the Remains of them are returned to their Den. Our People had none killed, three wounded, but none of them dangeroufly. The Number of killed and wounded of the Enemy not known.

Printed by J. CARTER.

273

BOSTON, 26th of JUNE, 1775.

THIS Town was alarmed on the 17th Inſtant at break of Day, by a Firing from the Lively Ship of War; and a Report was immediately ſpread that the Rebels had broke Ground, and were raiſing a Battery on the Heights of the Peninſula of Charleſtown, againſt the Town of Boſton. They were plainly ſeen, and in a few Hours a Battery of Six Guns, played upon their Works. Preparations were inſtantly made for the landing a Body of Men; and ſome Companies of Grenadiers and Light Infantry, with ſome Battallions, and Field Artillery; amounting in the whole to about 2000 Men, under the Command of Major General HOWE, and Brigadier General PIGOT, were embarked with great Expedition, and landed on the Peninſula without Oppoſition; under Cover of ſome Ships of War, and armed Veſſels.

The Troops formed as ſoon as landed: The Rebels upon the Heights, were perceived to be in great Force, and ſtrongly poſted. A Redoubt thrown up on the 16th at Night, with other Works full of Men, defended with Cannon, and a large Body poſted in the Houſes of Charleſtown, covered their Right; and their Left was covered by a Breaſtwork, Part of it Cannon Proof, which reached from the Left of the Redoubt to the Myſtick River.

Beſides the Appearance of the Rebels Strength, large Columns were ſeen pouring in to their Aſſiſtance; but the King's Troops advanced; the Attack began by a Cannonade, and notwithſtanding various Impediments of Fences, Walls, &c. and the heavy Fire they were expoſed to, from the vaſt Numbers of Rebels, and their Left galled from the Houſes of Charleſtown, the Troops made their Way to the Redoubt, mounted the Works, and carried it. The Rebels were then forced from other ſtrong Holds, and purſued 'till they were drove clear of the Peninſula, leaving Five Pieces of Cannon behind them. Charleſtown was ſet on Fire during the Engagement, and moſt Part of it conſumed. The Loſs they ſuſtained, muſt have been conſiderable, from the vaſt Numbers they were ſeen to carry off during the Action, excluſive of what they ſuffered from the ſhipping. About a Hundred were buried the Day after, and Thirty found wounded on the Field, ſome of which are ſince Dead. About 170 of the King's Troops were killed, and ſince dead of their Wounds; and a great many were wounded.

This Action has ſhown the Bravery of the King's Troops, who under every Diſadvantage, gained a compleat Victory over Three Times their Number, ſtrongly poſted, and covered by Breaſtworks. But they fought for their KING, their LAWS and CONSTITUTION.

274

ACKNOWLEDGMENTS

TEXT

The following printed works, which have been of special value in the writing of this story, are gratefully acknowledged here and strongly commended to all who would pursue this subject further:

The Declaration of Independence: Its History, by John H. Hazelton (New York: Dodd, Mead & Co., 1906)

The Declaration of Independence: The Evolution of the Text, by Julian P. Boyd (Princeton: Princeton University Press, 1945)

The Declaration of Independence: The Story of a Parchment, by David C. Mearns (Washington: Library of Congress, 1950)

The Declaration of Independence: A Study in the History of Political Ideas, by Carl L. Becker (New York: Alfred A. Knopf, 1951)

The Spirit of the Revolution, by John C. Fitzpatrick (Boston and New York: Houghton Mifflin Co., 1923)

Diary and Autobiography from *Works of John Adams,* edited by Charles Francis Adams, vols. II, III (1850)

Autobiography from *The Writings of Thomas Jefferson,* edited by Paul Leicester Ford, vol. I (1892)

The Autobiography of Benjamin Rush, edited by George W. Corner (Princeton University Press for the American Philosophical Society, 1948)

Dictionary of American Biography, vols. I-XX (New York: Scribners, 1928–36)

I also wish to thank my friend and former student, Dr. Albert Hall Bowman, for assistance in compiling materials about the Signers.

D. M.

PICTURES

ABOUT seven years ago we began our search for the pictorial material which has finally culminated in the publication of this book. During this period, we have met many people who, by their interest and knowledge, have helped us greatly. We should like to thank them at this time for their generous assistance and for making their collections available to us.

It is, unfortunately, impossible to list all the individuals who assisted in countless ways. Our debt of gratitude to them is immeasurable. Special mention, however, should be given to Charles Francis Adams, Boston; Mrs. Ronald V. C. Bodley, Boston; Elliott Muse Braxton, Hampton, Va.; Philip A. Carroll, Ellicott City vicinity, Md.; Mrs. George Vaughn Curtis, Arlington, Va.; Mrs. Morton Downs, Bryn Mawr, Pa.; Henry Middleton Drinker, Jenkintown, Pa.; Edward Eberstadt and Sons, New York; Henry C. Edgar, West River, Md.; Miss Frances J. Eggleston, Oswego, N.Y.; J. B. Harkrider, Shreveport, La.; Mrs. Alice Huger Hayden, Ocean Springs, Miss.; Mrs. T. Charlton Henry, Philadelphia; Mrs. Carlos A. Hepp, New York; Dr. Henry Laurens, New Orleans; Edward J. Lee, Chatham, Va.; Mrs. John Henry Livingston, Tivoli-on-Hudson, N.Y.; Dr. George E. McClellan, Woodstock, Conn.; three sons of Thomas Montgomery, Jr., Woods Hole, Mass.; Frederick S. Moseley, Jr., New York; Mrs. Charles James Murray, Strathcarron, Scotland; Mrs. John T. Nichols, Garden City, N.Y.; Mrs. R. W. Norton, Shreveport, La.; William A. Otis, Boston; Dr. John Randolph Page, New York; John B. Paine, Boston; Charles Coleman Sellers, Hebron, Conn.; Mrs. J. Madison Taylor, Philadelphia; Roger Wolcott, Milton, Mass.

American Philosophical Society, Philadelphia
The Baltimore Museum of Art, Baltimore (James W. Foster, Jr.)
Library of the Boston Athenaeum, Boston
Museum of Fine Arts, Boston (G. H. Edgell)
The Brooklyn Museum, Brooklyn
Carnegie Institute, Pittsburgh (John O'Connor, Jr.)
Cary Memorial Library, Lexington, Mass.
Connecticut State Library, Hartford (James Brewster)
Corcoran Galley of Art, Washington, D.C. (James Breckinridge)
Fogg Museum of Art, Cambridge (Arthur Pope)
Franklin and Marshall College, Lancaster, Pa.
Harris & Ewing, Washington, D.C. (Andrew J. May)
Henry E. Huntington Library and Art Gallery, San Marino, Calif.

Independence Hall, Philadelphia (Warren A. McCollough, M. O. Anderson)

Mariner's Museum, Newport News, Va. (Harold Sniffen)

Maryland Historical Society, Baltimore (James W. Foster)

Massachusetts Historical Society, Boston (Stephen T. Riley)

The Metropolitan Museum of Art, New York

National Archives, Washington, D.C. (Miss Josephine Cobb, Albert H. Leisinger, Jr., Karl Trever)

National Gallery of Art, Washington, D.C. (William P. Campbell, Charles C. Stotler)

National Portrait Gallery, London

The New Hampshire Historical Society, Concord, N.H.

The New Hampshire Society of the Colonial Dames (Mrs. Wallis D. Walker)

Chamber of Commerce of the State of New York

New-York Historical Society, New York (Arthur B. Carlson)

New York Public Library, New York (Miss Ramona Javitz, Ivor F. Hettich, Wilson G. Duprey)

The Old Print Shop, Inc., New York (Harry Shaw Newman)

Peabody Institute, Baltimore

The Pennsylvania Academy of the Fine Arts, Philadelphia (Mrs. Barbara S. Roberts)

The Historical Society of Pennsylvania, Philadelphia (R. N. Williams, 2nd)

Pennsylvania Hospital, Philadelphia

First Troop Philadelphia City Cavalry Armory, Philadelphia

Princeton University, Princeton (Donald D. Egbert)

Rhode Island Historical Society, Providence

Scottish National Portrait Gallery, Edinburgh, Scotland

Smithsonian Institution, Washington, D.C. (Jacob Kainen)

U.S. Capitol, Washington, D.C. (David Lynn, Edward H. King)

United States Naval Academy Museum, Annapolis (Captain Wade DeWeese)

The Valentine Museum, Richmond (Mrs. Ralph Catterall)

Virginia Historical Society, Richmond, (John Melville Jennings)

Virginia State Library, Richmond

Wadsworth Athenaeum, Hartford

Yale University Art Gallery, New Haven (Miss Elizabeth A. Livingston)

A special note of thanks to Mrs. McCook Knox of Washington, D.C., who, from the very beginning of our project, encouraged us and helped in the authentication of certain portraits.

We should like to give a special word of thanks to the following members of the Library of Congress: Frederick Goff, Rare Books Division; Dr. Percy Powell, Manuscripts Division; Donald Holmes, Chief of the Photoduplication Service, and the members of his staff: Mrs. Virginia Brooks, William E. Davis, Miss Olivera Durgy, Elmer King, Bernard J. McCarthy, Mrs. Jacquelyn Mitchell, and Ralph E. O'Hara. The fine work of the Photoduplication Service has enabled us to use many of the pictures which otherwise might not have been reproducible.

Our last, but by no means least, expression of appreciation is for Mrs. Henry W. Howell, Librarian; Miss Ethelwyn Manning, Honorary Librarian; and for the staff of the Frick Art Reference Library in New York, who have made our journey through the days of colonial portraiture most pleasant. The program of the Frick to acquire photographic negatives of American art in private collections and information relating to American art in public institutions has virtually made it a union catalogue of American art, a development for which we, and others who have used the files, are truly grateful.

H. M.
M. K.

PICTURE SOURCES

81 The manner in which the American colonies declared themselves independent of the King of England. Engraving in Edward Barnard, *The New, Comprehensive and Complete History of England* (1783). Courtesy Library of Congress.

82 Colonel John Nixon. Painting by Gilbert Stuart, *c.* 1800. Courtesy The Pennsylvania Academy of the Fine Arts, Philadelphia.

La Destruction de la statue royale à Nouvelle Yorck. Etching by Basset, 1780 (?). Courtesy Library of Congress.

83 Raising the Liberty Pole. Engraving by John C. McRae, 1875, after painting by F. A. Chapman. Courtesy Library of Congress.

87 The unanimous Declaration of the thirteen United States of America. Engraving by William J. Stone. Courtesy Library of Congress.

89 Timothy Matlack. Painting by Charles Willson Peale, *c.* 1779. Courtesy National Gallery of Art, Mellon Collection, Washington, D.C.

90 Signatures of John Hancock. Larger signature is from the Declaration of Independence, smaller signature from a letter dated 21 November, 1776. Courtesy Library of Congress.

91 The Declaration of Independence. Painting by John Trumbull, 1787–95. Courtesy Yale University Art Gallery, New Haven.

95 John Hancock's Defiance. Detail from lithograph by Currier & Ives, 1876. Courtesy Library of Congress.

97 State seals on this and the following pages are engravings by George Murray taken from the engraving of the Declaration of Independence published by John Binns in 1818. Courtesy Library of Congress.

98 Josiah Bartlett. Pencil drawing by John Trumbull. Courtesy The New Hampshire Historical Society, Concord.

99 The grave of Josiah Bartlett, Kingston, New Hampshire. Photograph by Hirst Milhollen, 1947.

The home of Josiah Bartlett, Kingston, New Hampshire. Photograph by Hirst Milhollen, 1947.

100 William Whipple. Painting by Ulysses D. Tenny after John Trumbull. Courtesy The New Hampshire Society of the Colonial Dames, Portsmouth.

101 The home of William Whipple, Portsmouth, New Hampshire. Photograph by Hirst Milhollen, 1947.

102 Matthew Thornton. Painting, artist unknown. Courtesy The Pennsylvania Academy of the Fine Arts, Philadelphia.

103 The grave of Matthew Thornton, Thornton's Ferry, New Hampshire. Photograph by Hirst Milhollen, 1947.

104 A prospect of the colledges in Cambridge in New England. Engraving by William Burgis, *c.* 1725–26. Courtesy Library of Congress.

106 John Hancock and his wife, Dorothy Quincy Hancock. Painting by Edward Savage, *c.* 1788. Courtesy Corcoran Gallery of Art, bequest of Woodbury Blair, Washington, D.C.

107 View of the seat of His Excellency John Hancock, Esq., Boston. Engraving by Samuel Hill in *The Massachusetts Magazine*, July 1789. Courtesy Library of Congress.

108 Order of procession, for the funeral of the late Governor Hancock. Broadside. Courtesy The New York Public Library, New York.

109 Samuel Adams. Paintings by John Singleton Copley, 1770–74. Courtesy the City of Boston. Photograph courtesy Museum of Fine Arts, Boston.

110 The grave of Samuel Adams, Old Granary Burying Ground, Boston, Massachusetts. Photograph by Hirst Milhollen, 1948.

112 John Adams. Painting by Mather Brown, 1788. Courtesy Library of the Boston Athenaeum, Boston.

113 The birthplace of John Adams, Quincy, Mass. Photograph by Hirst Milhollen, 1947.

115 Abigail Adams. Painting by Ralph Earle, 1785. Courtesy Miss Frances J. Eggleston, Oswego, N.Y.; photograph courtesy Harry Shaw Newman, The Old Print Shop, Inc., New York.

116 Robert Treat Paine. Painting by Edward Savage. Courtesy Estate of Charles J. Paine. Photograph courtesy Museum of Fine Arts, Boston.

119 Elbridge Gerry. Drawing by John Vanderlyn. Courtesy Fogg Museum of Art, Harvard University, Cambridge, Mass.

120 The birthplace of Elbridge Gerry, Marblehead, Mass. Photograph by Hirst Milhollen, 1948.

122 Stephen Hopkins. Detail of painting, Declaration of Independence, by John Trumbull in United States Capitol. Photograph courtesy Library of Congress.

123 Home of Stephen Hopkins, Providence, Rhode Island. Photograph by Hirst Milhollen, 1948.

124 William Ellery. Painting by James Reid Lambdin after John Trumbull. Courtesy Independence Hall, Philadelphia.

126 Yale College in 1749. Engraving by Thomas Johnston, 1749. Courtesy The New York Public Library, New York.

127 Roger Sherman. Painting by Ralph Earle. Courtesy Yale University Art Gallery, New Haven.

Home of Roger Sherman, New Haven, Connecticut. Lithograph in William Brotherhead, *The Book of the Signers*, 1861. Courtesy Library of Congress.

128 Oliver Wolcott. Painting by Ralph Earle. Courtesy Connecticut State Library, Hartford.

129 Mrs. Oliver Wolcott (Laura Collins). Painting by Ralph Earle. Courtesy Roger Wolcott, Milton, Mass. Photograph courtesy Frick Art Reference Library, New York.

130 William Williams. Painting by John Trumbull, 1778. Courtesy Dr. George E. McClellan, Woodstock, Conn.

131 Mrs. William Williams. Detail from painting by John Trumbull, 1778. Courtesy Dr. George E. McClellan.

The home of William Williams, Lebanon, Connecticut. Photograph by Hirst Milhollen, 1948.

132 Samuel Huntington. Painting, artist unknown. Courtesy Connecticut State Library, Hartford.

133 The home of Samuel Huntington, Norwich, Connecticut. Photograph by Hirst Milhollen, 1948.

134 The grave of Samuel Huntington, Norwich, Connecticut. Photograph by Hirst Milhollen, 1948.

136 Francis Lewis. Engraving by Charles Cushing Wright in John Sanderson. *Biography of the Signers to the Declaration of Independence*, 1824. Courtesy Library of Congress.

137 Trinity Church, New York. Lithograph by John Forsyth, 1847. Courtesy Library of Congress.

138 Philip Livingston. Painting by Benjamin West. Courtesy Mrs. John Henry Livingston, Tivoli-on-Hudson, New York. Photograph courtesy Frick Art Reference Library, New York.

139 The Brooklyn home of Philip Livingston. Reproduction of pen and ink drawing in *Magazine of American History*, December 1885. Courtesy Library of Congress.

140 Mrs. Philip Livingston (Christina Ten Broeck). Painting by Benjamin West. Courtesy Mrs. John Henry Livingston. Photograph courtesy Frick Art Reference Library, New York.

141 Lewis Morris. Painting by John Wollaston, *c.* 1755. Courtesy National Gallery of Art, Mellon Collection, Washington, D.C.

142 Mary Walton Morris. Painting by John Wollaston, *c.* 1755. Courtesy National Gallery of Art, Mellon Collection, Washington, D.C.

Home of Lewis Morris, Morrisania. Wood engraving in *Magazine of American History*, June 1892.

143 William Floyd. Painting by Ralph Earle. Courtesy Mrs. John T. Nichols, Garden City, Long Island, N.Y.

144 The home of William Floyd, Westernville, New York. Photograph by the Fitchard Studio, Rome, N.Y.

146 John Hart. Painting, artist unknown. Courtesy Independence Hall, Philadelphia.

147 The grave of John Hart, First Baptist Churchyard, Hopewell, New Jersey. Photograph by Hirst Milhollen, 1948.

148 John Witherspoon. Painting by Charles Willson Peale, *c.* 1783. Courtesy Princeton University, Princeton, N.J.

149 A northwest prospect of Nassau Hall with a front view of the President's House in New Jersey. Engraving by H. Dawkins in *An Account of the College of New Jersey*, 1764, after W. Tennant. Courtesy Library of Congress.

150 The home of John Witherspoon, Princeton, New Jersey. Photograph by Hirst Milhollen, 1948.

151 The grave of John Witherspoon, Princeton, New Jersey. Photograph by Hirst Milhollen, 1948.

152 Richard Stockton. Painting attributed to John Wollaston. Courtesy Princeton University, Princeton, N.J.

153 Mrs. Richard Stockton (Annis Boudinot). Painting attributed to John Wollaston. Courtesy Princeton University, Princeton, N.J.

The home of Richard Stockton. Wood engraving in Martha J. Lamb, *Homes of America*, 1879. Courtesy Library of Congress.

154 Abraham Clark. Miniature by James Peale. Courtesy Henry C. Edgar, West River, Md.

155 The home of Abraham Clark. Lithograph in William Brotherhead, *The Book of the Signers*, 1861. Courtesy Library of Congress.

The grave of Abraham Clark, Rahway, New Jersey. Photograph by Hirst Milhollen, 1948.

156 'My days have been so wondrous free.' Manuscript. Courtesy Library of Congress.

190 Charles Carroll. Painting by Thomas Sully, 1833–34. Courtesy the State Capitol, Annapolis.

191 Doughoregan Manor, Ellicott City vicinity, Maryland. Photograph by Hirst Milhollen, 1954.

193 Chapel of Doughoregan Manor, where Charles Carroll is buried. Photograph by Hirst Milhollen, 1954.

194 William Paca. Painting by Charles Willson Peale, 1772. Courtesy Peabody Institute, Baltimore. Photograph courtesy Frick Art Reference Library, New York.

195 The home of William Paca, Annapolis. Photograph taken before 1890. Courtesy Historic American Buildings Survey, Library of Congress.

196 The home of Samuel Chase, Annapolis. Photograph by Hirst Milhollen, 1947.

197 Samuel Chase. Painting by Charles Willson Peale, c. 1773. Courtesy Maryland Historical Society, Baltimore. Photograph courtesy Frick Art Reference Library, New York.

198 Mrs. Samuel Chase (Anne Baldwin) and daughters, 1772–75. Painting by Charles Willson Peale. Courtesy Maryland Historical Society, Baltimore. Photograph courtesy Frick Art Reference Library, New York.

199 Thomas Stone. Painting by Robert Edge Pine. Courtesy The Baltimore Museum of Art, Baltimore.

200 Habre-de-Venture, the home of Thomas Stone, near Port Tobacco, Maryland. Photograph by Frances Benjamin Johnston, 1935. Courtesy Library of Congress.

The grave of Thomas Stone, Habre-de-Venture, near Port Tobacco, Maryland. Photograph by Hirst Milhollen, 1947.

202 College of William and Mary: Brafferton Hall, Christopher Wren building, President's House. Detail from the Bodleian Plate. Courtesy Library of Congress.

203 Richard Henry Lee. Painting by Charles Willson Peale, c. 1795–1805. Courtesy Edward J. Lee, Chatham, Va. Photograph courtesy Frick Art Reference Library, New York.

204 Stratford, Westmoreland County, Virginia, the birthplace of Richard Henry Lee. Photograph by Hirst Milhollen, 1946.

205 Thomas Jefferson. Plaster bust by Jean Antoine Houdon. Courtesy The New-York Historical Society, New York.

207 Monticello, Virginia, the home of Thomas Jefferson. Photograph by Hirst Milhollen, 1946.

208 Drawing by Thomas Jefferson for his tombstone. Manuscript. Courtesy Library of Congress.

209 The grave of Thomas Jefferson, Monticello, Virginia. Photograph courtesy Library of Congress.

210 Benjamin Harrison. Detail from painting, Declaration of Independence, by John Trumbull, in the United States Capitol. Photograph courtesy Library of Congress.

211 Berkeley, Charles City County, Virginia, the home of Benjamin Harrison. Photograph by Hirst Milhollen, 1948.

212 George Wythe. Miniature by Henry Benbridge. Courtesy Mrs. R. W. Norton, Shreveport, La.

213 The home of George Wythe, Williamsburg. Photograph by Hirst Milhollen, 1947.

215 Francis Lightfoot Lee. Painting, artist unknown. Photograph courtesy Harris & Ewing, Washington, D.C.

Menokin, home of Francis Lightfoot Lee, Warsaw vicinity, Virginia. Photograph by Frances Benjamin Johnston about 1935. Courtesy Library of Congress.

216 Carter Braxton. Painting, artist unknown. Courtesy Elliott Muse Braxton, Hampton, Va.

217 Elsing Green, Virginia, the home of Carter Braxton. Photograph by John Beckstrom, 1936. Courtesy Historic American Buildings Survey, Library of Congress.

218 Thomas Nelson, Jr., as a young boy. Painting by Mason Chamberlain. Courtesy Dr. John Randolph Page, New York. Photograph courtesy Frick Art Reference Library, New York.

219 The Thomas Nelson house, Yorktown, Virginia. Photograph by the Detroit Photographic Company, 1905. Courtesy Library of Congress.

220 The Thomas Nelson house, Yorktown, Virginia. Watercolor by Benjamin Henry Latrobe, c. 1796. Courtesy Virginia State Library, Richmond.

222 Joseph Hewes. Painting by Charles Willson Peale, 1776. Courtesy United States Naval Academy Museum, Annapolis.

223 Monument erected to the memory of Joseph Hewes, Courthouse Green, Edenton, N.C. Photograph by Hirst Milhollen, 1948.

224 John Penn. Miniature by Charles Willson Peale. Courtesy Mrs. R. W. Norton, Shreveport, La.

The home of John Penn, Stovall vicinity, North Carolina. Lithograph in William Brotherhead, *The Book of the Signers*, 1861. Courtesy Library of Congress.

225 William Hooper. Detail from painting, Declaration of Independence, by John Trumbull, in the United States Capitol. Photograph courtesy Library of Congress.

226 Statue of William Hooper, Guilford Courthouse National Military Park, Guilford County, North Carolina. Photograph by Hirst Milhollen, 1948.

228 The Temple, London, England. Engraving in John Stow, *A Survey of the Cities of London and Westminster, and the Borough of Southwark*, 1754. Courtesy Library of Congress.

229 Arthur Middleton, his wife Mary Izard, and son Henry. Painting by Benjamin West, 1771. Courtesy Henry Middleton Drinker, Jenkintown, Pa. Photograph courtesy Frick Art Reference Library, New York.

230 Middleton Place, Charleston vicinity, South Carolina, a wing of the home of Arthur Middleton. Photograph by Hirst Milhollen, 1948.

The grave of Arthur Middleton, Middleton Place, South Carolina. Photograph by Hirst Milhollen, 1948.

231 Castillo de San Marcos, St. Augustine, Florida. Photograph by Hirst Milhollen, 1948.

232 Thomas Heyward, Jr. Painting by Jeremiah Theus. Courtesy Mrs. Alice Huger Hayden, Ocean Springs, Miss. Photograph courtesy Frick Art Reference Library, New York.

233 Mrs. Thomas Heyward, Jr. (Susanna Savage). Painting by Edward G. Malbone. Privately owned. Photograph courtesy Frick Art Reference Library, New York.

The home of Thomas Heyward, Jr., Charleston, South Carolina. Photograph by Hirst Milhollen, 1948.

234 The home of Edward Rutledge. Lithograph in William Brotherhead, *The Book of the Signers*, 1861. Courtesy Library of Congress.

235 Edward Rutledge. Painting, artist unknown. Courtesy Dr. Henry Laurens, New Orleans, La. Photograph courtesy Frick Art Reference Library, New York.

236 Thomas Lynch, Jr. Miniature by John Ramage. Courtesy Mrs. R. W. Norton, Shreveport, La.

237 Mrs. Thomas Lynch, Jr. (Elizabeth Shubrick). Painting, artist unknown. Courtesy Mrs. J. Madison Taylor, Philadelphia. Photograph courtesy Frick Art Reference Library, New York.

Hopsewee, Santee, South Carolina, the birthplace of Thomas Lynch, Jr. Photograph by Hirst Milhollen, 1948.

238 Siege of Savannah, 1779. Contemporary map. Courtesy Library of Congress.

240 Lyman Hall. Wood engraving in William Hunt, *American Biographical Panorama*, 1849. Courtesy Library of Congress.

241 Signers Monument, Augusta, Georgia, where Lyman Hall and George Walton are buried. Photograph by the Detroit Photographic Company, 1905. Courtesy Library of Congress.

242 Button Gwinnett. Detail from lithograph, Signers of the Declaration of Independence, published by Ole Erekson, 1876. Courtesy Library of Congress.

243 The duel in which Button Gwinnett was killed by Gen. Lachlan McIntosh. Lithograph in William Brotherhead, *The Book of the Signers*, 1861. Courtesy Library of Congress.

Button Gwinnett house, St. Catherine's Island, Georgia. Photograph courtesy private collection.

244 George Walton. Miniature by Charles Willson Peale, *c.* 1772. Courtesy Mabel Brady Garvan Collection, Yale University.

245 Meadow Garden, Augusta, Georgia, the home of George Walton. Photograph by Frances Benjamin Johnston. Courtesy Library of Congress.

248 Detail from photograph of textile. Courtesy Library of Congress.

249 Back of the State House, Philadelphia. Engraving by William Birch & Son, 1799. Courtesy Library of Congress.

250 Old Courthouse, York, Pennsylvania, where the Declaration was kept from September 1777 to July 1778. Wood engraving in W. C. Carter and A. J. Glossbrenner, *History of York County, from Its Erection to the Present Time*, 1834. Courtesy Library of Congress.

A front view of the State-House, etc., at Annapolis the Capital of Maryland. Engraving in *The Columbian Magazine*, February 1789. Courtesy Library of Congress.

251 A view of Broad Street, Wall Street, and the City Hall. Watercolor, probably by John Joseph Holland, 1797. Courtesy The New York Public Library, New York.

252 Georgetown and Federal City, or City of Washington. Aquatint by T. Cartwright, 1801, after drawing by G. Beck. Courtesy Library of Congress.

253 The taking of the city of Washington in America. Woodcut published by G. Thompson, 1814. Courtesy Library of Congress.

254 A view of the President's House in the City of Washington after the conflagration of the 24th August 1814. Aquatint by William Strickland after drawing by George Munger. Courtesy Library of Congress.

Department of State. Engraving in John Howard Hinton, *The History and Topography of the United States*, 1830. Courtesy Library of Congress.

255 Tyler facsimile subscription book. Courtesy of Edward Eberstadt and Sons, New York.

256 Declaration of Independence. Engraving designed and published by John Binns in 1818. Courtesy Library of Congress.

257 Patent Office, Washington, D.C. Daguerreotype by John Plumbe, Jr., c. 1845. Courtesy Library of Congress.

258 Independence Hall, Philadelphia, 1876. Lithograph by Thomas Hunter, 1876. Courtesy Library of Congress.

Interior view of Independence Hall, Philadelphia. Lithograph by Louis N. Rosenthal. Courtesy Library of Congress.

259 Fireworks at the Washington Monument on July 4th. Photograph courtesy Andrew J. May, Harris & Ewing, Washington, D.C.

260 Young America. 'Celebrating the Fourth.' Lithograph by Currier & Ives, 1867. Courtesy Library of Congress.

American Independence. Lithograph by C. C. Brainard, 1859. Courtesy Library of Congress.

Fireworks in the Country. Wood engraving in *Harper's Weekly*, July 10, 1869, after drawing by C. G. Bush. Courtesy Library of Congress.

261 The picnic on the Fourth of July. Engraving by Samuel Hollyer & John Rogers, 1864, after Lilly M. Spencer. Courtesy Library of Congress.

Richard Henry Lee, of Virginia, reading the Declaration of Independence at Independence Square, July 4, 1876. Wood engraving in *Frank Leslie's Illustrated Newspaper*, July 22, 1876. Courtesy Library of Congress.

Fireworks photograph by The Strimbans. Fireworks made available through courtesy Rene D. Lyon Company, New York.

262 The Declaration of Independence being transferred to a Library of Congress truck, September 30, 1921. Photograph by Herbert E. French. Courtesy Library of Congress.

263 President and Mrs. Calvin Coolidge at the dedication of the Shrine in the Library of Congress, which housed the Declaration of Independence and the Constitution of the United States, February 28, 1924. Photograph by Herbert E. French. Courtesy Library of Congress.

The Shrine, Library of Congress. Photograph courtesy Library of Congress.

264 Roy W. Wampler, Alvin Kremer, and Dr. Gordon E. Kline and the final sealing in of the Declaration of Independence at the Bureau of Standards, Washington, D.C., June 18, 1950. Photograph courtesy Library of Congress.

265 The Declaration of Independence and the Constitution of the United States leaving the Library of Congress for the National Archives, December 13, 1952. Photograph courtesy National Archives, Washington, D.C.

Removal of the Declaration of Independence from the Library of Congress to the National Archives, December 13, 1952. Courtesy Library of Congress.

The installation of the Declaration of Independence at the National Archives, Washington, D.C. Photograph courtesy the National Archives.

267 The shrine in the National Archives containing the Declaration of Independence and the Constitution of the United States. Photograph courtesy the National Archives.

269-274 Broadsides are from the collections of the Library of Congress.

285

# of Text & Pictures

287